THE
PUZZLING ADVENTURES OF
DR. ECCO

DENNIS SHASHA

Department of Computer Science
Courant Institute of Mathematical Sciences
New York University

D1021806

DOVER PUBLICATIONS, INC.
Mineola, New York

Bibliographical Note

This Dover edition, first published in 1998, is a corrected and revised republication of the work first published by W.H. Freeman and Company, New York, in 1988.

Library of Congress Cataloging-in-Publication Data

Shasha, Dennis Elliott.
    The puzzling adventures of Dr. Ecco / Dennis Shasha.
        p.   cm.
    "Revised and corrected republication of the work first published by W.H. Freeman and Company, New York, in 1988"—T.p. verso.
    Includes bibliographical references and index.
    ISBN 0-486-29615-6 (pbk.)
    1. Mathematical recreations.   I. Title.
QA95.S47   1998
793.7'4—dc21   97-43592
                                           CIP

Manufactured in the United States of America
Dover Publications, Inc., 31 East 2nd Street, Mineola, N.Y. 11501

*To Claude Shannon, Michael Rabin,
and Tek Young Lin*

Contents

Acknowledgments

These puzzles have come from many sources and many people. Almost like a novel, they reflect life experiences. Much credit goes to the following people:

my wife Karen who helped shape both the text and the figures, and whose insights and wit are always fresh;

my parents, my sister Carol, and my brother Robert who showed me many worlds, then let me choose;

Carrie Pete whose organization and good sense have taught me so much;

the Singer family, especially Loren, whose good advice, generous friendship, and inspiring writing were crucial in bringing this book about;

my friends, teachers, and colleagues at IBM, Harvard, and Courant whose suggestions and approaches have influenced this book, especially Brad Barber, Richard Cole, Larry Denenberg, John Giraldi, Paul Heintz, Bill Nohilly, Michael Overton, Paul Spirakis, Stuart Tucker, Myron Zajac, and the Dreishpoons;

my agent Jonathan Wells, editor Jerry Lyons, project editor Susan Moran, designer Nancy Field, and the many other talented people at Freeman who helped make this manuscript into a book;

and, of course, J. E., whom I hope to see again soon.

Preface

Dr. Jacob Ecco is a mathematical detective and puzzle solver. In this book he helps his clients discover treasures, outsmart kidnappers, and identify spies by means of deduction and insight. His clients' puzzles are meant for you to solve as well. Dr. Ecco is accompanied by Professor Scarlet, who asks questions and records their adventures. Scarlet's remarks and questioning will help you work toward your own solutions.

The puzzles are inspired by the methods and thinking of researchers in computer science and mathematics. They require no special background in either subject, but solving them will lead you to some central ideas in the two fields.

You have to like challenges. Some puzzles have stumped physicists, a psychiatrist, and several computer science colleagues of mine for a long time. On the other hand, an artist I know well (my wife, Karen) has solved most of them. You don't need training, only a clear head and imagination.

The table of contents rates the puzzles according to their level of difficulty. As the difficulty rating goes from A to D, the more ingenuity you need to solve the puzzle. Throughout the episodes and adventures in the book you are asked to think about and provide solutions. The direct questions to you are marked by a magnifying glass. Have fun.

Dennis Elliott Shasha
Courant Institute of Mathematical Sciences
New York University

Preface to the Dover Edition

Though I loved mathematical puzzles as a child, it was only at IBM that I realized they might help me keep my job. Just out of college, I was hired to design circuits for a large mainframe. The most challenging ones to design were circuits to check the correctness of other circuits. The goal was to design a machine that could diagnose itself.

While turning these problems over in my mind, I felt myself lost in the details of electrical levels, circuit fanouts, and heat dissipation. So, I decided to abstract the problem into a puzzle that I could, in principle, explain to any smart person, whether engineer or not. Once framed that way, a friend and I solved the puzzle and then I was able to design the circuit. (See Circuits Checking Circuits)

A few years later, when I was in graduate school, Michael Rabin's algorithm course seemed to be pushing me to the limits of my ability to think. I managed to convert some algorithms to puzzles that captured most of their essential ideas. (See The Tower of Lego, The Coach's Dilemma, Rocket Assembly, Delicate Balances and Warehouses and Barrels). I then was able to add in the details and program them.

Shortly after that, I met a young artist named Karen. I knew it was serious when she solved a difficult problem (Party) in a few minutes and another one (The Camper's Problem) in seconds. Even my professor colleagues take longer. It is in the hopes that many smart readers will enjoy and profit from puzzles that I welcome this Dover edition of my book.

The Dover edition of this book has benefited from the corrections of many dedicated readers of the Freeman edition, especially Andy Liu and his students. Other sharp readers include Aaron Brown, E. Browning, Fred Galvin, Andrew Palfrey, and Arthur Protin who made helpful suggestions.

Dennis Shasha
Courant Institute of Mathematical Sciences
New York University

Introduction

Everybody has heard of Jacob Ecco nowadays, particularly since Presidente Carballero bestowed his country's highest honors on him. But who would have guessed that this young man, now barely thirty, would have achieved fame as a puzzle solver?

Everyone who knew Ecco as a boy expected him to become a prominent academic mathematician. It was hard to avoid such an expectation. Ecco received his Ph.D. from Harvard at age nineteen with a thesis called *Combinatorial Catastrophe Theory*. It was an extraordinary unification of two hitherto disparate fields and has become the basis for much research since then. But Ecco refused all offers of employment. He dropped out of academic life, moving to MacDougal Street in New York City's Greenwich Village. He called himself an *omniheurist*—a person who solves all problems. Over the next ten years, he became a world famous puzzle solver with a global clientele.

So much is common knowledge. What is surprising is that few people know much more. How did Ecco get started? What puzzles has he solved besides the famous ones? How hard are they? What is Ecco really like? The truth is that I don't know the complete answers to these questions, but I believe I know more than anyone else—aside from Ecco, of course.

You see, Ecco and I have been chess companions and friends over six of the last ten years. During that time I have kept records of our conversations and the puzzles that have come to him. He has consented to let me publish my records provided that I present the facts of each puzzle as he himself learned them.

"Only thinkers will like my story," he explained to me. "And thinkers will want to solve the puzzles themselves."

Ecco's "story" began for me when he was still a boy (as was I). I was in a baker's shop, eyeing the cinnamon cookies carefully. A woman came in with her son. Both had unruly reddish hair. The boy had huge eyes, with white around the pupils, giving the impression of a state of alarm or anger. The two were engaged in a heated discussion about music. The boy argued that chorales could be made much more exciting with augmented fourths. The mother said that augmented fourths were forbidden in chorales by the church, which called them the "devil's interval." The boy stuffed his hands in his pockets and hunched his shoulders. "Rules, rules," he said, "too many arbitrary rules."

The baker seemed to know the woman and her son, and he smiled as they approached. The boy suddenly became preoccupied by a large carrot cake with a well-cooked crust and a thin layer of soft vanilla icing on top. It was sitting alone on the long cutting board behind the counter.

The mother gave her order for bread, but the boy kept looking at the cake. The baker noticed this and made an extraordinary offer.

"I'll give you your bread for free if you can solve the following little problem," said the baker. "Tell me how I can cut this cake into sixteen equal pieces using four straight cuts." *(Try it.)*

This started me thinking. I had heard about a solution to a similar problem with three cuts giving eight pieces. But sixteen pieces, that seemed tough.

The boy answered almost immediately. "How many solutions would you like?" he asked.

"One would be enough, but remember that everybody has to get icing," said the baker.

"Oh, yes," replied the boy. "You're right, there is only one solution really. You cut the cake in four pieces using two cuts at right angles to one another. Then you line them up and cut down the middle, giving you eight pieces. Lining them up one more time gives sixteen."

"Right, Jake," said the baker. "You get the cake, too."

The mother tried to insist on paying, but the baker refused. "It is always a pleasure to see the young Jacob Ecco, especially now that he is about to go off to college."

The boy and mother thanked him and left (with the cake).

They were still discussing music, but on much more friendly terms.

College? I thought. The kid can't be more than twelve, unless he's some sort of midget. But college it must have been. Jacob Ecco began studying mathematics at Harvard at thirteen.

The incident haunted me through high school. It was so bizarre and unresolved. Who was that kid? *Where* was he? I would have thought I'd see him at a chess tournament, but I never did.

When my time came to go off to college, I thought I was doing well, studying philosophy, linguistics, and finally information theory at Yale. I'm not sure how I would have felt had I known that young "Jake" had already received his Ph.D. in mathematics by the time I was a junior.

It was in graduate school that our one-way acquaintanceship resumed. One of my teachers, a great theoretician from Hungary, was quoting a remarkably clever result in combinatorics and attributing it to one Jacob Ecco. It couldn't be the same person, I thought. But I was wrong. Ecco had completed his thesis four years earlier. It had become a classic and was the basis for much active work in computer science and in mathematics, though in arcane parts of those fields.

What had happened to Ecco then? I scanned the journals, seized by the idea that this person was the "Jake" in question. But I found nothing by him at all. When I asked my Hungarian professor, he shook his head, his eyes lowered, saying, "He disappeared, he just disappeared."

The next time I saw Ecco in person was at a seminar on algebraic topology four years later at the Institute for Mathematical Sciences in New York City. The speaker had just presented a complicated conjecture, assuring us that it was true, though he still had to work out the details. By this time I myself was a professor, but I was far from seeing how the proof would go. A man in blue jeans walked to the podium and handed the speaker a piece of paper. "Your conjecture is false," he said, and then he walked out of the room.

There was a commotion at the speaker's platform. The speaker read the page and flushed bright red. It contained a two-line counterexample to the conjecture.

A few weeks later, I saw the speaker again. He told me that the person who had handed him the paper was none other than Jacob Ecco. And Ecco had sent a letter apologizing for his behavior and suggesting a weaker theorem with a simple proof. The theorem was all the speaker needed for his other results.

I told the speaker that Ecco resembled a young boy I had once seen in a bakery in Chelsea. His curly red hair on top of a huge head, long straight nose, huge angry-looking eyes, and thin frame struck me as exactly what an adult version of the boy should look like. "Not hard to believe," said my colleague. "He's lived in this area since he was a kid—except when he was at Harvard. If you visit, warm him up by talking chess."

I went to his MacDougal Street apartment that very day. He looked at me rather impatiently as he opened the door, but he began smiling and joking as soon as we began talking about chess. When I asked him about the bakery, he confirmed that he went there often as a child. The baker often gave him puzzles. He did remember the carrot cake.

"I ate it too fast and got sick," he said smiling. His smile turned suddenly into a frown. "Poor mother," he said more to himself than to me. "Her only child gets his Ph.D. and she dies within days of a sudden, freak heart attack. I was all set to go to Bell Labs, but I couldn't go. Instead I went to Italy, renting an apartment in San Gimigniano overlooking vineyards. Every morning the roosters woke me up and I sat by the window watching the sun rise.

"Finally, I decided to move here, near the chess players, your mathematics institute, and jazz. I also decided to study the last terrestrial frontier, the brain." His apartment was jammed with neurobiology texts and journals, as well as almanacs, government registries, and mathematics books. There was also a shelf with volumes on anthropology, cognitive psychology, and philosophy.

I asked him how he earned his living. "I solve puzzles," Ecco said. "My clients include governments, artists, journalists, and paupers."

"Is there any connection between your puzzle solving and your brain work?" I asked.

"Absolutely," he answered. "Part of my work is to study the

experimental literature and to theorize about the brain. But part of my theorizing comes from looking at myself solving puzzles. What are the steps of reason? What are the leaps of insight? What kinds of problems are easy for people to solve and what are hard? I have reason to believe that puzzle solving plays a large role in our thinking processes, though not necessarily puzzles of the level of difficulty that I relish."

I looked for Ecco's articles in the neuroscience literature, but couldn't find his name. Once I met a neuroscientist who said that he hadn't heard of Ecco but that I should look at the paper by one John Eliot, who had just published a mathematical theory of memory that explained a class of experiments, including some strange results about forgetting.

Having read Ecco's thesis, I immediately recognized the style: a disarming beginning, followed by a provocative mathematical theory, followed by solid experimental support. It was like Ecco not to use his own name. I've never seen anyone so publicity shy.

Ecco smiled when I asked him about the paper. "I hope you liked it," he said. I never saw him write a paper and rarely saw him read. He always seemed to work with a felt-tipped pen on scraps of paper, often nibbling at a cookie, or he would lie down and stare at the ceiling.

Our early meetings evolved from chess gossip to chess playing. Often clients would come in and I would hear them present their problems, which Ecco might solve as they waited. But often we would just talk and play chess. Ecco was very private, but from time to time he would become positively expansive. I always took advantage of the occasion to ask him personal questions. The one that was initially most on my mind was why he just didn't take a research job and do puzzles on the side.

"Think about it. In almost any time before the twentieth century, there was no support structure for researchers, writers, or artists," he answered. "There were a few patrons, but their support was fickle at best. Johann Sebastian Bach, for example, had financial troubles throughout his life, and his wife was buried in a pauper's grave.

"Yet every generation seems to create about the same amount of true greatness. Our time gives scientists wonderful support, yet great theories are just as sparse as ever. They are often lost in the din of pretended theories and hollow hypotheses. That's what I realized when I was communing with those roosters in San Gimignano. Graduate school had nearly led me to mistake noise for thought. Maybe I'll return, but I want to solve a few real problems first."

A NOTE TO TEACHERS

Professor Andy Liu of the University of Alberta has developed a university-level course based on Dr. Ecco. He has written a book titled Professor Scarlet's Notebook containing explanatory text and problems extending those found in The Puzzling Adventures of Dr. Ecco.

He and his colleagues have used the two books over several semesters to teach combinatorics and the students both enjoy the approach and learn a lot. If you are interested in ordering or examining Professor Scarlet's Notebook, please contact Professor Liu at the following address:

Professor Andy Liu
Department of Mathematics
632 Central Academic Building
University of Alberta at Edmonton,
T6G 2G1, Canada
email: mathdept@sirius.math.ualberta.ca
fax: 1-403-492-6826
phone: 1-403-492-3396

CHAPTER ONE

Eccentrics

—①—
MINORITY RULES

Vote early and vote often.
— *unattributed.*

It was one of those clear, cold February Sundays when even New York stays inside, yielding for once to the weather. Ecco greeted me at his door. "Won't you have some tea?" he said, indicating the pot on the table.

As I poured the tea, Ecco asked, "So, did you read the news about the vote scandal in the Patagonian Congress?"

"Briefly," I said. "I don't much care about the Congress." The Patagonian Congress is an international association of scientists, government bureaucrats, and business executives that advise the United Nations.

"But, my dear Professor," replied Ecco, "it was an outstanding example of the illogic of the press: it was reported as such, but actually there was no scandal."

"Who told you that?" I asked, surprised that Ecco would have any contacts in the political world.

"I figured it out," he said. "Look at what the *Times* says. 'There were three candidates for the presidency of the Congress, Guarez, Swenson, and Libretti. Before the election, Guarez and his archenemy Swenson were each reportedly backed by more than 40 percent of the members. That left Libretti with less than 20 percent, probably because of the widely held view that he had no vision and was too naive. Yet Libretti won the election. Outside observers conjecture that there must have been some trickery, but members of the Congress refuse to discuss it.'

"Now, Professor, other newspapers have picked up the story

13

and reported it as if rumors of a stolen election were established fact. But I happen to have the Patagonian congressional bylaws here, and I believe that the election abided entirely by the rules. You see, the bylaws provide for presidential races to proceed by a series of elections, each between only two candidates. Thus, the first election could be between Guarez and Swenson, the second between the winner of that and Libretti. Or, the first election could be between Swenson and Libretti, and the second between the winner of that and Guarez. Or, finally, Libretti and Suarez could face each other in the first election. In any case, there are two one-on-one elections."

 Before reading on, do you see how Libretti could have won the presidency honestly?

Ecco continued. "The bylaws change everything. Because of the emnity between Guarez and Swenson, no matter what order the election occurs in, Libretti wins. The supporters of Swenson prefer him to Guarez. The supporters of Guarez prefer him to Swenson."

A few days later, a letter to the editor appeared in the *Times* expressing this same argument; it was signed only K. Arrow. The letter itself was quoted by the news wire services. I could see Ecco's style in the letter, but Ecco just said, "No, the credit goes all to Arrow."

"I sense an admission in your denial," I said.

Ecco smiled. "Well, perhaps there is," he replied. "Remember how Kenneth Arrow jolted the world of social science with his so-called Possibility Theorem? Among other things, the theorem shows that the preferences of the majority can be subverted by multiway elections — that is, elections in which more than two candidates face off at the same time.

"For example, Arrow showed that under some election schemes a candidate who can beat any other candidate in a one-on-one election — such a person is sometimes called the Condorcet candidate — might still lose. Suppose there are three candidates, A, B, and C; A is far to the right, C far to the left, and

B middle of the road. If a runoff system is used, the two highest vote getters in the first election compete in the second election. If the electorate is highly polarized, as it was in the Patagonian Congress, then B would be knocked out in the first election. However, B, would beat either A or C in a one-on-one contest.

"The election protocol in the Patagonian Congress was set up to ensure that the Condorcet candidate, if there is one, always wins. The only assumption is that voters are true to their preferences in every election. The press assumed the bylaws required multiway elections. That's why they considered Libretti to be a sure loser."

No sooner had the words left Ecco's lips than we heard a knock at the door.

Antonio Libretti, the new president of the Patagonian Congress, certainly didn't strike me as a man with little vision. On the contrary, he seemed a man of clear-cut goals and cogent reasons for them.

"So, you see, gentlemen," Libretti concluded his remarks, "what is at stake is the future of the Amazon and possibly our planet. The bill I support and wish to see the Congress pass would limit further development there, whereas the competing proposals would all lead to encroachments on the jungle that would be impossible to stop."

Ecco nodded, though unenthusiastically. "Mr. Libretti, your goals are most worthwhile and I am all for them, but you said that your problem required my services. I am certainly no lobbyist."

"I know, Dr. Ecco. It is not a lobbying service but a logical problem I have come to discuss with you. To begin, let us abstract all of the proposals concerning the Amazon into letters: A, B, C, and D. My proposal is C. Of the others I prefer A to D and D to B.

"There are 100 members of the Patagonian Congress and 17 of them share exactly my preferences. There are 32 who prefer A to B, B to D, and D to C. There are 34 who prefer D to B, B to C, and C to A. There are another 17 who prefer B to A, A to C, and C to D."

"If I may summarize, Mr. Libretti," said Ecco, "you have described the preferences in order as follows:

(C, A, D, B); 17 supporters
(A, B, D, C); 32 supporters
(D, B, C, A); 34 supporters
(B, A, C, D); 17 supporters

The first group represents you and your 17 supporters, who prefer C to A, A to D, and D to B, and similarly for the other groups."

"Yes, exactly," said Libretti. "Now, as you can see, my position finds little favor among most Congress members. Moreover, I can't even vote. But I have one privilege that I hope to use to my advantage.

"Our system stipulates that the winner among several choices must be determined by a sequence of one-on-one elections. For example, the first election might pit A against B. The second might pit the winner against C, or C against D, and so on. Of course, only the winner of an election may participate in any further ones. When only one choice remains, that choice is the winner. However, the form of the elections can affect the outcome, as you have already observed in your analysis of my election."

Ecco started. After all, how could Libretti know that Ecco was responsible for the current analysis of Libretti's election?

"My prerogative as president," Libretti continued, "is to choose the ordering of the one-on-one elections."

"And you think that your proposal is going to win that way?" I asked. "If you were representing B, I could see that you had some hope. But C? In an election between B and C, B would win 83 votes. C is certainly no Condorcet candidate."

Libretti turned to me and frowned. "If you and Dr. Ecco put your heads to it, I'm sure you'll find a way," he said.

 (1) Assuming that each person votes according to his or her preferences each time, is there any sequence of one-on-one elections that would make C the winner? If so, what is it? (Solution on page 139.)

"Well, Mr. Libretti, here is your answer," said Ecco, handing over a sequence of one-on-one elections. "You can pass the resolution to save the Amazon. The reason this works is that there is no Condorcet candidate, so the order can make a difference."

"Excellent," said Libretti. "Just one more point of concern: the tradition in multiway contests like this one is that the president selects the two participants in the first election, but that the opposition suggests the pair standing for the second election. In this case, the opposition are the people whose first choice is B or D. The question is: If I choose in the first election and the opposition chooses in the second, can I guarantee that one of my first two choices, C or A, will win?"

(2) Can you ensure that C or A will win if you choose the first pair of proposals and your opposition chooses the second? Recall that subsequent elections may use winners only from their predecessors. If your answer is yes, say what proposals should stand for the first election. You must show that C or A will then win no matter which pair is chosen for the second election. If not, why not?

"Tradition is still a wonderful thing," said Libretti after hearing Ecco's answer. With a smile, he shook hands with us and left.

"Well," said Ecco, turning to me after Libretti had left, "do the ends justify the means, Professor? We've made Libretti and his tiny minority win, thus subverting what should be a democratic process. But maybe the funny rule of one-on-one elections is the cause of it all."

(3) Show that any of A, B, C, or D can win given an appropriate ordering.

"People surely underestimated Libretti to call him naive," I said. "He is willing to resort to great shrewdness to get what he wants, good though it may be."

"Or, maybe they understood a deeper sense of naive," said Ecco. "Imagine the backlash when people see that Libretti has used the voting system to his advantage again. He may then lose his fragile support." Ecco paused, his chin resting on his palm with his eyes fixed on the floor. "Then again, people may decide that he is an overpowering force and jump on the bandwagon." Ecco smiled and sighed. "If only politics were as easy to understand as mathematics."

—②—

THE TOWER OF LEGO

Ecco already had many clients when I first began to visit him. But a question kept gnawing at me: How did he start his practice as an omniheurist—a profession so new he had to coin the name of it? How could he ever convince anyone to become his client? It seemed quite mysterious to me. But to Ecco, finding his market was merely another puzzle to solve.

"A person in any freelance profession eventually gets clients through references or fame," Ecco explained when I finally mustered the courage to ask. "Early on, prospective clients must be, first, willing to risk the unknown, and, second, they must have no alternative. The first condition precludes timid corporate and government bureaucrats. The second implies that prospective clients would need only the slightest encouragement to seek me out. Desperate people seize at every hope, no matter how farfetched. Look at the wild success of religious charlatans.

"I therefore placed a short advertisement in the classified sections of carefully selected periodicals. These included international newspapers and alumni magazines of certain universities. I have placed the advertisement barely two dozen times in my career. Word of mouth has done the rest."

Ecco gave me a copy of his advertisement. It read:

Puzzle solver available.
Solves real-life problems of mathematical nature.
XYZ MacDougal Street, New York City

"Seems a bit brief," I observed. "But you say it worked?"

"Splendidly," said Ecco. "But not without some mishaps. One magazine balked at publishing such an 'enigmatic' advertisement. They demanded a copy of my Ph.D. diploma before they would publish anything suggesting mathematical expertise. (I had finished my schooling by then.) Another magazine omitted the word 'mathematical' and I began to get inquiries from people trying to overcome life crises. I recommended a trip to San Gimigniano."

One of Ecco's first clients was an eccentric, the famous millionaire Hank Alfred. Ecco told me the story with some amusement.

"It was a Sunday afternoon and I still lived in a graduate student dorm. I was hot on the trail of a combinatorial proof when I was aroused by several loud knocks, apparently made by a cane. When I opened the door, an elderly gentleman walked in with a decisive stride. His cane was a walking stick, but he held it in his hand like a scepter.

"'Jacob Ecco, my name is Hank Alfred,' he said, shaking my hand vigorously. 'I plan to mark my name in history if it's the last thing I do. I want to build a tower that is a kilometer high,' he continued. 'I'd like to do it fast, in a year if possible. I don't care so much if anyone lives in the tower, just that it's built. I have the land (flat desert), the technology, and the money. Now I only need the method. If you can help me, Ecco, you'll be a wealthy man.'

"I liked Mr. Alfred immediately, and the problem sounded like great fun. My only worry was that I would find myself in Ripley's *Believe It or Not*. But Mr. Alfred assured me of anonymity.

"'You see, Ecco,' he continued, 'there are these prefabricated building units that pile up on one another like my granddaughter's Lego pieces. Each of them is 100 meters long and 100 meters wide, but only 1 meter tall, a large square. On their top and bottom, they have couplers that allow them to be connected

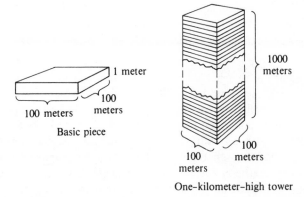

Figure 1   By stacking 1000 blocks, the millionaire Hank Alfred
intends to build a tower 1 kilometer high.

with one another. My engineers say that we could stack them
10,000 high if we wanted. They are so lightweight that a special
lifter can grab the bottom square of a stack of 5000 squares and
place that stack on top of another one. I can provide you with as
many lifters as you need. Now, putting one square on top of
another one takes a week. Putting one stack on top of another
also takes a week, but if either of the stacks is more than 100 tall,
it takes an additional week to set things up. I will spare no
expense. How fast is the fastest it can be done?'"

 (1) *Using unlimited resources, starting with just the
unstacked squares, how fast can a crew build this vertical
kilometer? State the schedule you propose. (Solution on
page 139.)*

"After I told him, he leaned on his elbow and thought for
some time. 'That's pretty fast,' he said. 'Tell me. What if we tried
to build a 10-kilometer tall building? How long would that
take?'"

 (2) *How long would it take to get 10 vertical kilometers,
again starting from scratch?*

"I gave him his answer. He was as good as his word. He built his monument as discreetly as such a colossus can be built. My name never appeared in any of his press releases."

—③—
ODD DOORS PROBLEM

Proofs are chess games laid out in words.
   —*from Ecco's notebook, "Views of Mathematical Thinking."*

By the time our acquaintance began and Ecco was established, his clients were often wealthy and eccentric. Well, sometimes they themselves weren't eccentric, but then they had distinctly eccentric forbears. That was the case with the client who visited Ecco's apartment one spring morning.

"Dr. Ecco, my name is Lawrence Terrence III," the young blond man said as he entered. He had one of those accents whose geographical boundaries are islands around a few prep schools. "I am wealthy," he continued, "but I may soon be a poor man without your help. That is a sad fate in my part of Kentucky.

"You see, my father recently passed away. He left his substantial collection of jewels in a chest in one of two underground labyrinths that he built during his lifetime. The trouble is that he didn't tell me where the jewels are except that they are in a room with an odd number of doors. He told me that I should be able to figure out which labyrinth contains the jewels.

"The trouble is that I haven't a clue. Both labyrinths are completely flooded with brackish water and silt, so sending a crew down either one will cost nearly a million dollars. Dr. Ecco, I'd very much appreciate it if you would tell me which labyrinth I should look in."

Ecco appeared puzzled for a moment, then sank into thought. I didn't think the young man have given him enough information. Then Ecco lifted his head suddenly and said, "Tell me more about the labyrinths. Do you know anything about the connections between the rooms?"

The young man said, "The doors are all perfectly normal, connecting two different rooms. To tell you the truth, I'm beginning to think my poor father was crazy and there are no jewels, though he never deceived me before. He was an amateur mathematician, an interest that I tried to acquire but never seemed fit for."

Ecco continued his questions. "How many doors are there for entering or leaving the labyrinths?"

"The first labyrinth has two entrance doors and the other has three. Father always seemed to be eccentric, but, as I said, he was an amateur mathematician."

"What do you think, Professor?" Ecco asked me. "If Mr. Terrence's father was telling the truth, then only one of these labyrinths has any rooms with an odd number of doors. Suppose we can prove that one of them *must* have a room with an odd number of doors. That would have to be the one holding the jewels. I was puzzled at first because I thought that only a mathematician would realize that the answer is, in fact, unambiguous. But the late Mr. Terrence was a mathematician."

"Mr. Terrence," Ecco continued speaking to the young man, "here is the labyrinth you should go to."

 Which labyrinth must have a room with an odd number of doors? Can you prove it? (Solution on page 140.)

"Dr. Ecco," said Terrence, barely understanding the explanation. "I hope you're right. If you are, you can be sure, I'll be forever grateful."

Ecco smiled as he accompanied his guest to the door. "Gratitude is the most undependable of emotions," he said to me with a sarcastic chuckle after Terrence had left.

Ecco's cynicism was unwarranted, at least in this case. Shortly after the newspapers published a photograph of young Terrence standing aside a large open chest of jewels, Ecco received a handsome check and the following note:

Dear Mr. Ecco,

I should never have doubted you. Here is a small token of my gratitude. If you come to Kentucky for the races, please consider this an open invitation to my house.

L.

—④—
THE COACH'S DILEMMA

I have endeavored, whenever possible, to give a hint of Ecco's life and thoughts. In a way that I can't fully justify, understanding his way of thinking — his cynicism and his idealism, his toughness and his complaints — are vital to understanding his approach to puzzles. It all comes down to his study of ideas and their permanence.

One of the ideas that he has often repeated to me is his insistence on reducing problems to their simplest components. "I always try to solve the simplest nontrivial instance of a problem and try to generalize from there," he would say. "Often the generalization is easy. When it isn't, I'm probably thinking the wrong way about the simple problem." Ecco applied this principle to the problem of Coach McGraw.

It was a late spring evening and we were listening to Bach solo cello suites. The doorbell rang, introducing a man with a deep tan and a sports jacket over a freshly washed sweat suit. He was very agitated.

"Which one of you is Dr. Ecco?" he asked. After Ecco introduced us both, he said, "My name is Ed McGraw and I am the coach for the Olympic tennis team.

"Yesterday my top-ranking team members were all injured in a freak plane accident. They will recover soon, but I need to prepare substitutes tomorrow to play England's team. I know who the eight members of my substitute team will be, but I must rank them in a day.

"So far, I've been able to get just one court to play on. I want to set up singles matches of one hour each among the players in such a way that I can figure out who is best, who is second best, and so on, up until who is eighth best. I was going to use an old-fashioned tennis ladder, but that always seems to take a week to sort itself out. I need to do it all within 20 hours. Dr. Ecco, can you tell me what to do?

Ecco thought a few moments. Then he asked, "May we assume, Mr. McGraw, that if player X beats player Y and Y beats Z, then X would beat Z if they played?"

"Well, that's not always true, but if you need to, then assume it," said McGraw. "Also, you should know that the players are in good shape and any one of them is capable of playing a few matches in a row."

"Well then, Mr. McGraw, I've got good news for you. You can rank your eight players from best to worst in less than 20 hours, provided that every match takes just one hour. Here's how."

 (1) Try to find a solution that works no matter what the outcome of a particular match. Ecco found one that works in 17 hours. (Solution on page 141.)

"You see, Coach McGraw," Ecco said as he finished the explanation, "the key is to break down the problem into its simple components. Anyone can solve your problem for two players. From that, four is not too hard. From two groups of four, eight wasn't too difficult either."

Coach McGraw thanked Ecco and left. Ecco and I began a long chess game, which Ecco opened with the king's gambit. He blundered badly toward the end, and I saw that he was preoccupied.

After he conceded the game, he leaned on his left arm and began scribbling on paper. "You know, professor, it is strange," he said after some time. "The method I proposed to the coach won't help him much if he gets more courts. Yet the method I would suggest if he had more courts would be very bad if he only had one."

As he finished speaking, the phone rang. It was McGraw. "Dr. Ecco, sorry to call so late, but we have been given four courts. Trouble is, using your method with several courts, it still takes eleven hours. Can't we do better? I need to get this over with as quickly as possible."

Dr. Ecco seemed relieved to get the call. "Mr. McGraw, I suspected you might phone. You can finish the entire ranking process in six hours if you have four courts. To start with, pair off the players and have each pair play at a court. After that, I will tell you what court the winner and loser of each match should go to in the next hour or whether he should rest."

 (2) What is a solution that works in six hours using four courts? Remember, your solution must work no matter who wins in each hour. (This is hard.)

"It's not all that different from your first solution," I pointed out to Ecco later. "Again, you rank pairs, then fours, and then all eight."

"The principle of solving the simplest nontrivial case still applies," said Ecco. "The troubling thing is that six hours are necessary. In my solution, there are two hours in which only two courts are used. Could we rank the players in five hours, I wonder?"

 (3) Do you think it's possible to rank the players in five hours? (An unsolved puzzle.)

A month later, Ecco received a plaque with a tennis racket and an Olympic symbol on it. He turned to me after looking at the plaque. "Tell me, professor, do you think I'll ever find my face on a cereal box, encouraging young aspiring athletes to eat shredded starch?"

—⑤—

MAXIMUM FLOW

Perhaps the affair of the Patagonian Congress has given the impression that Ecco is an avid reader of newspapers. But nothing could be further from the truth. His interest is more aroused by demographic shifts in China than by political pronouncements. Often he does without daily newspapers altogether, relying on weeklies, feature magazines, and scholarly reviews for his knowledge of world developments.

That's why I was so surprised when I saw him huddled over the daily newspaper one evening studying the damage pattern of the recent Siberian earthquake. The reason for his interest turned out to be purely professional.

"The oil fields were near the epicenter," he observed. "Perhaps that explains the phone call from Houston that I found on my answering machine."

Before I could ask what he meant, the phone was ringing again. I picked up the extension as usual. A shipper of oil drilling equipment was on the phone. "Dr. Ecco," he said, "our customers in Moscow want us to deliver 20 tons of equipment by tomorrow evening. The equipment is ready in Houston now. Unfortunately, the airlines don't have much room left.

"The maximum capacities between now and tomorrow evening are:

Houston to Frankfurt — 3 tons
Houston to Paris — 11 tons
Houston to Rome — 3 tons

Houston to London — 10 tons
Rome to Moscow — 13 tons
London to Warsaw — 8 tons
Frankfurt to Warsaw — 4 tons
London to Paris — 2 tons
Paris to Frankfurt — 10 tons
Paris to Moscow — 2 tons
Frankfurt to Moscow — 8 tons
Warsaw to Moscow — 7 tons

"Can we get the 20 tons to Moscow by tomorrow evening, and if so how?" The shipper hung up after begging Ecco to call back with the answer as soon as possible.

Ecco looked at me as I was jotting down calculations. He sat back staring at the ceiling. A few minutes later, I handed Ecco my conclusion.

"Quite right, Professor," he said as he read my suggested flows along each route. "I have been working on the answer to the next question."

The phone rang. I was trying to figure out what the next question might be. "Well, Dr. Ecco?" asked the shipper, too impatient to wait for the call.

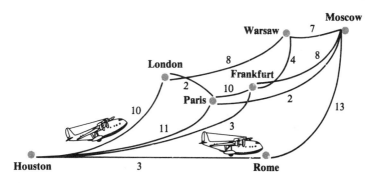

Figure 2 Capacities in tons along air routes from Houston to Moscow.

"You can do it, sir. Here are the shipment amounts along each route, compliments of Professor Scarlet," Ecco said, smiling at me.

 (1) What are the shipment amounts? (Solution on page 145.)

"Thank you, doctor," said the shipper. "The truth is, though, we want to ship more. What is the maximum we could get through?"

Ecco smiled. "Precisely the question I expected. Well, it's a nice round number, I assure you."

"But, Dr. Ecco, how can you be so sure?"

 (2) What is the round number? What reasoning would you have used?

"I see," said the caller. "One more question . . . ." I have to admit to being pleased that Ecco hadn't predicted this one.

"Assuming we can charter four planes and send 3 tons per plane, which routes should we add them to in order to increase the maximum tons shipped by a total of 12?"

 (3) Which existing routes should they add planes to?

Ecco answered, and the caller thanked him. A few days later a package containing a gold replica of a drill rig housing was hand-delivered to Ecco. In it was a note:

Dear Dr. Ecco,
    This is a one-of-a-kind drilling rig. I send it as a Texan's token of appreciation for your help.

"Trinkets for the rich and famous," said Ecco as he put the rig inside a shoebox and in the far reaches of his closet. "Still, it might come in handy some day."

—⑥—
CRITICAL PATHS

Because Ecco spends much of his time solving problems with only pencil and paper, most people think of him as an unathletic sort. Although he is not in the 'body-building movement' ("Why should body building be dignified with the term 'movement'?" I heard him mutter once), he is an avid swimmer, skier, and, most of all, a windsurfer.

"It's hard to hurt yourself windsurfing," he told me one morning. "Falling usually just means hitting the water. But you can drown if you're not careful.

"One day in Salem, the wind picked up until it was much stronger than I could handle. By the time I realized this, I was two miles from land. The wind had risen just as my muscles were getting very tired. I managed a water-start with great difficulty. I hooked into my harness and felt a jolt of acceleration as I aimed the board toward the shore. The wind shifted slightly; the sail caught a gust and flew to leeward. The harness carried me with the sail. I found myself in that most humiliating of positions— sail flat over the water and me sprawled face down on top of it. The wind seemed to blow harder over my head as I climbed back onto the board. I remember thinking that the wind was toying with me. The thought made me angry. But then maybe it wasn't even bothering to toy with me. Maybe I was beneath its notice. That was frightening."

It didn't sound like all that much fun to me and my face must have shown it.

"You shake your head, Professor, but I treasure that day in my own perverse way," Ecco continued. "It is easy to forget nature altogether here in New York. Our shelters are stronger than the weather. Stormy days on the sea belie that manmade hubris."

Not being as worried about hubris as Ecco, I didn't feel so tempted to try the sport. But Ecco said that usually there was no significant danger and it was marvelous fun. Anyway, Columbia Gorge on the West Coast had a shore on two sides. Barely reassured, I nevertheless accepted Ecco's invitation to accompany him and his windsurfing companion, Evangeline Goode, across the country to Portland, Oregon, and then up the river to the Gorge.

Evangeline was a philosopher in her late twenties who studied nonmonotonic logics at Princeton. Her dress was more bohemian than scholarly, and she had the stride and physique of a dancer. During the plane ride to Oregon, we discussed countless logical problems having to do with falsifying conclusions upon the introduction of new axioms. Once we landed and were driving to the Gorge, however, Ecco and Evangeline engaged in a nonstop discussion of wind conditions, sails, and hulls.

Gradually I learned Evangeline's story. She was the daughter of an American missionary doctor and a Manchurian nurse. Her family left after the revolution in China and moved to Montana. Evangeline grew up riding horses and fishing trout, like many young Montanans. What was different was her startling academic success. She won prize after prize, both national and international. Stanford gave her a full scholarship and a living stipend, Oxford awarded her a Rhodes, and Princeton granted her a fellowship. None of the schools seemed bothered by her concentration in a seemingly obscure discipline. Maybe they knew that the obscurity would soon yield to her seminal papers applying nonmonotonic logic to artificial intelligence and quantum mechanics.

The day after we arrived, Ecco woke me up for an early breakfast and a land lesson on the physics of windsurfing. He and Evangeline gave me a board with a long tether to a buoy. After about an hour of falling, I went back to our cottage, thoroughly exhausted. A long nap refreshed me, and I was all set to try again, when the phone rang.

"This is Mr. Henderson's secretary. Are you Dr. Ecco?" the voice asked.

"No, he is engaged," I said, thinking that windsurfing might not be a proper activity for an omniheurist. I also wondered how this Henderson knew where we were.

"Very well," said the voice. "Please tell Dr. Ecco that Mr. Henderson will call on him this evening."

Before I could protest or ask to check with Ecco, the caller disconnected. I told Ecco about the call when he and Evangeline returned. He just smiled. "The rich are different from you and me, Professor. They don't ask for appointments."

Mr. Henderson arrived in a car almost too wide and long to navigate our driveway. The man who emerged was tall and silver-haired. He evaluated our cottage with a few sweeping glances and then walked toward the doorway.

When he entered, he made straight for Ecco and laid out his story. "My advisers say it is going to take six and one-half years," he said, as he ended his story. "But that is too long, Dr. Ecco, way too long. We must be able to finish in four and one-half years at the most. I'm willing to put my entire fortune at the disposal of this task, although I would like some of it for my retirement."

Dr. Ecco turned to me. "Mr. Henderson, I'd like you to meet my friends, Professor Scarlet and Professor Goode," said Ecco. Henderson shook our hands forcefully, but his mind was elsewhere.

"As you have heard," Ecco explained to us, "Mr. Henderson is supporting the construction of an institution for the study of noncarbon life forms. The construction entails the completion of six tasks, which we will call A, B, C, D, E, F. But these tasks are interdependent in the following ways.

"Each of B and C takes four years. A takes two years but cannot begin until B is completed. F takes three years and D takes four, but D cannot begin until F is at least half done. E also takes three years but cannot begin until D is half done."

"Yes, I see that it will take at least 6.5 years," I said. I then presented a sequence of tasks that had to take at least 6.5 years, given the dependencies among the tasks.

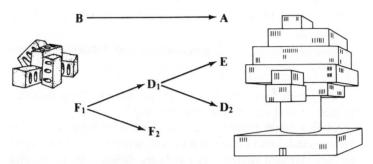

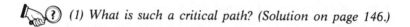

Figure 3 Six interdependent tasks must be completed to build the Institute for Noncarbon Life Forms. D consists of D_1 (first half and D_2 (second half). Similarly, F consists of F_1 and F_2.

(1) What is such a critical path? (Solution on page 146.)

Henderson continued. "Well, my advisors tell me that for five million dollars, any single task can be completed in half the time allotted, and for ten million dollars in quarter the time. What is the least I can pay to get the whole thing done in four and a half years?"

(2) What do you say and how would you do it?

Ecco resolved Mr. Henderson's problem in short order (beating the requirement by a half year). Then he turned to our guest and asked, "How long have you had me followed?"

Henderson didn't even blush. "Oh, a few months," he said. "You don't go out very often, but many people come to you and call you up. I've checked the backgrounds of a good number of men. When I saw your solution of the Terrence case, I was impressed, but I figured it might be luck. It was my friend Hank Alfred who really convinced me. Still, I delayed. Your coming out to Oregon left me with no excuse, however, so I had my secretary set up the appointment. How do you know that I have had you followed?"

"I inferred you were having me followed when Professor Scarlet told me of your call," Ecco said. "I had told no one of my trip. Also, you came directly to me when you came in. I figured you had to have seen pictures."

"You're right," said Henderson. "Incidentally, I'm not the only one. My agents have told me that certain security agencies have been checking on you as well."

Mr. Henderson left. Ecco was clearly not happy. He seemed preoccupied the rest of the evening, refusing discussions of any sort. Evangeline explained that the first day at the Gorge was always tough on Ecco, so Mr. Henderson's revelation might not have been the only cause of his reticence. Fortunately, the wind and weather were superb for the rest of our stay. After our week was up, Ecco was much more composed.

We were all smiling as we approached Ecco's door back in New York. But Ecco's smile fell when he put his key in the door. "Someone has come in. I never double-lock my front door," he said.

We rushed into the apartment, but nothing was missing and nothing seemed to have been moved. I began to think that perhaps Ecco had double-locked the door accidentally.

"You might think I'm mistaken," said Ecco reading my thoughts, "but look at this."

He showed me a piece of paper. On it was written a strange message:

nwjq udwnwj sjwf'l qgm?

CHAPTER TWO

First Spies

—①—
SPIES AND ACQUAINTANCES

Ecco's feelings about spy organizations are a mixture of fascination with the danger and intrigue they exude, fear of their powers of surveillance, and contempt for the incompetence they often hide behind a mask of secrecy. Following our windsurfing trip and the discovery of the coded message, suspicion of surveillance was uppermost on his mind.

In fact, a change had come over Ecco. His privacy had been violated. His profession, which had heretofore provided him with great independence, was now the reason he was kept under surveillance. He began to show some strain.

"When an explosive detonator enters the city, some law enforcement agency knows about it and commonly asks for a warrant, according to a district attorney I know," said Ecco. "Now think about it. How do they know about the detonator? What technology could they have at their disposal? These very comments are probably being bugged," Ecco added angrily.

He even went so far as to buy an eavesdropper detector, but he was unable to find anything.

Ecco's first visitor from the intelligence community came within a month after our Oregon trip. He identified himself only as a government official.

"We have captured several people whom we suspect are part of a spy ring," he said after perfunctory introductions. "For security reasons, I will identify them as A, B, C, D, E, F, and G. "We have interrogated all seven. A admits to having met the other six. B admits to having met five, C to having met four, D to having met three, E to having met two, F to having met two, and G to having met one.

"None of them would identify whom they knew, but at least we got the numbers out of them. No spy would claim to have met more people than he has actually met, since the interrogation would then be very hard on him if he couldn't come up with critical information.

"Our lie detectors are hard for most people to fool so normally we would think that they're all telling the truth. Could they be?"

"First tell me whether your sophisticated electronics are bugging my apartment," Ecco demanded.

"You may rest assured, Dr. Ecco, that we aren't doing anything of the sort. I would not be talking this freely if I thought your apartment was bugged," our visitor answered.

"Well, the answer to your question is no," said Ecco, satisfied for the moment.

 (1) How did Ecco know the spies were not all telling the truth? (Solution on page 147.)

"That was our conclusion, too," said our visitor. "In that case, probably at most one person has met more of the others than he says. As I said, very few spies can fool our lie detectors. We would prefer not to waste our effort with a more intensive interrogation of all of them. We've already done so with F and are convinced that he is telling the truth. Can you figure out who is lying just from the information I've given you? If not, can you tell me who is telling the truth for sure?"

Ecco thought for some time. "I'm afraid that there are a few remaining suspects. Here are the people I know are honest," he said at last.

 (2) Who is honest for sure? Assume that F is telling the truth and there is only one liar.

Ecco presented his conclusions. Our visitor thanked us and started to leave, placing an envelope stuffed with money on the table by the door of the apartment. He was stepping out when Ecco said abruptly, "Keep your payment sir. Just call off your snoops."

Our visitor turned around and stepped back into the room, leaning against the door. "Dr. Ecco, you've become too important to us," he said with a patronizing smile. "I am only the first of many who will come to you for help. The other side may start to employ you. We must protect our interests."

"I'm not sure I believe that," said Ecco, "but even assuming I do, what if I don't want to be protected?"

"We must protect our interests, Dr. Ecco," the visitor repeated.

"What if I refuse to help you any further?" Ecco asked.

"That is a possibility. But we've studied you quite carefully, Dr. Ecco. It is hard for you to resist challenging problems, and we have a wealth of those," said our visitor.

"True," Ecco said. "It's the same snare you use on academics. Though one can disagree with some of your goals, your problems are irresistable."

"Anyway, our surveillance will decrease drastically. We have absolute trust in you personally." The visitor looked at us both, turned, and left.

"Do you think he's telling the truth about not bugging me?" Ecco wrote on a piece of paper after the man had left.

I shrugged and tore up the paper.

SPIES AND DOUBLE AGENTS

Ecco has been visited by many more security agencies since that first time. Unfortunately, I am not at liberty to report on most of them. Those that do appear have been "sanitized." For this I beg the reader's understanding.

One of our more frequent visitors was a gentleman of distinguished though gruff bearing, who came to be known by us as "the Director." The Director never revealed his true name. When he called, there were always strange noises in the background, supposedly to foil eavesdroppers.

So, when the phone interrupted our chess game one day, I wasn't surprised that Ecco picked up the receiver, recognized the noises, and said, "Oh, Paul, how are you?" Ecco had taken a perverse interest in exposing the secrets, even the most innocent ones, of the security agencies.

"Old trick," said the Director in annoyance. "Maybe my name is Paul and maybe it isn't."

"I'm sure, Mr. Director," replied Ecco. "Perhaps I should try the name of your dog next time. You do have a dog, or is that classified?"

"Listen, Dr. Ecco, we have a major national security problem. There is no time for jokes."

"Sorry, Mr. Director. At your service."

The Director began. "We just got some reports from two spies, but we don't understand what they've sent. Also, one may be a double agent. You see, one of our agents recently was shot, and in his dying breath he said that only one of these two spies was trustworthy, but he didn't know which one."

"Be so kind as to come to my apartment tomorrow, Mr. Director, and we will see what we can do," said Ecco.

The Director's facial muscles were drawn tight when he came in the next day. "Another agent was shot. I'm worried that the untrustworthy spy is responsible."

Ecco tried to be reassuring. "First let's see the messages."

The Director handed them to Ecco who made some comments in the margins. He smiled briefly, then nodded and began to scribble.

"Your spies are logicians I see," said Ecco. "Do you mind if I show Professor Scarlet? I will abstract the real contents, of course."

The Director nodded reluctantly. Ecco used to call him the Secret Miser. It was certainly true that he hated giving away any information.

"Professor," said Ecco to me, "each of the letters W, X, Y, and Z stands for assertions that are either true or false. I'll call the spies A and B." Then Ecco told me what they said.

Spy A reported:

Exactly one of W, X, and Y is true.
Exactly one of X, Y, and Z is true.
Exactly one of W and Z is false.

Spy B reported:

Exactly one of W, X, and Y is true.
Exactly one of X, Y, and Z is true.
Exactly one of W, Y, and Z is true.

"Well, Director," Ecco said as he completed his scribblings, "here are two pieces of paper. The first contains the name of the untrustworthy spy, and the other contains the assertion or assertions that the trustworthy spy's report suggests are true."

 Which spy is lying and which spy is telling the truth? Which assertion or assertions must be true? Try to present a convincing proof. (Solution on page 148.)

The Director looked at the first piece of paper. He blanched. "But he was my college roommate! I've known him for years. Prove that he lied."

Ecco smiled and handed him a third piece of paper. "There is your proof, Mr. Director." Dr. Ecco turned to me and let out a contented sigh. "Ah, Professor, isn't it good to hear that the guardians of our national security are well educated. Perhaps our kind director will tell us whether he feels loyal to blue, crimson, or orange."

"Too bad you're so smart, Ecco," the Director muttered ominously as he left.

─③─
ROCKET ASSEMBLY

A man in his early forties, William Noholly had unruly light brown hair. He entered the room with a light stride, wearing a jacket that was too tight and a tie that didn't match.

"Which one is Dr. Ecco?" he asked. Ecco extended his hand and then introduced me.

"Glad to meet you," said Noholly. "Listen, Doc, we've got a problem. The Feds want us to design a new factory to make spaceship control rockets. They want us to build the rockets all on a single factory floor. There are several subassemblies in the development of rockets. The subassembly stations are connected by conveyor belts. Because of problems we've had in other factories, we don't want any one conveyor belt to pass over another one. The darn bridges we have to build when that happens always give us grief.

"Let's call the subassemblies A, B, C, D, E, F, G, H, I, and J. Here is how they're related:

> At C, we need subassemblies A and B. So we'll need conveyor belts from where A and B are assembled to the station for C.
>
> To construct D, we need C and F.
> To construct E, we need B and D.
> To construct G, we need E and A.
> To construct H, we need B and G.
> To construct I, we need F and H.
> To construct J, we need I.
> J is the final station.

From J, fully assembled rockets go to the loading docks.

"Doc, can you figure out a way to design the conveyor belts without using crossover bridges? We want every assembly to happen in one place. For example, we don't want some of the E's to be produced in one place and others in some other place."

(1) Is what Noholly wants possible? If you say yes, draw a layout that works. (Solution on page 148.)

Noholly nodded to indicate that he had understood Ecco's answer. "One more question, Doc," he said. "It turns out that the output of D is fuselages, and they can be useful on their own. If we produce both the rockets and the fuselages, we'll need conveyor belts from both D and J to the docks. Can we get both rockets and fuselages out to the loading docks without any bridges? We might have to produce 'basic items' A, B, and F in more than one place. But reproducing a basic item assembly station costs five million dollars, so don't use too many."

"Do there also have to be conveyors from the loading docks to A, B, and F?" Ecco asked.

"Well, not for B," said Noholly. "The components for B are so small that we can bring them in when the factory is not running and have enough for several days. So we don't need a conveyor from the loading docks to B assembly sites."

(2) Give a solution that requires as few basic item construction stations as possible and that produces both fuselages (assembly D) and rockets (assembly J) without any bridges.

Ecco wrote down the solution in diagram form. Noholly studied it and nodded enthusiastically. Then he loosened his tie, got up and stretched, and asked, "Are you boys interested in something to drink?"

To my surprise Ecco accepted and even went so far as to invite Evangeline, who was visiting a colleague to discuss research. Ecco, Noholly, and Evangeline had a drinking contest. Ecco ended up sound asleep, Noholly singing ballads, and Evangeline calmly telling me about her research.

—④—
OFFSHORE OIL WELL

The journal *Oil and Gas* published a short article about Ecco's role in the Siberian resupply operation, although Ecco had not cooperated at all with the journalist. "The next thing you know, international oil speculators will ask me to predict the market for light crudes," he muttered as he skimmed the article.

Ecco refused many clients over the next few weeks, but the case of the offshore oil well with the two-way pipe proved too seductive.

Laura Austin introduced herself as an engineer from a Louisiana-based oil supply company. "Dr. Ecco," she said, "we are designing an off-shore oil rig to pump oil at a rate of one barrel per minute. The equipment on the rig consumes fresh water at a rate of about 0.1 barrel per minute. The rig has a 100-barrel oil drum and a 10-barrel water drum.

"We would like to build a single pipe from the shore to the drilling rig, carrying water out and bringing oil in. Our filters prevent the oil or water from going to the wrong destination, so there is no problem using the same pipe for both, but we can't pump both ways at the same time.

"To change over from oil to water takes six minutes from the time when the last oil leaves the drilling rig to the time when the first water leaves the shore. Six minutes is also the time to change from water to oil.

"The question is, how many barrels per minute does the pipe have to be able to handle in order to keep the storage drums from overflowing and to keep sufficient water on the rig? Also, how often should we switch from water to oil and back again?"

 (1) What is the necessary capacity of the pipe? How often should the company switch between water and oil? (Solution on page 150.)

"I am a student of New York City intersections, Ms. Austin," said Ecco. "Your problem bears a strong resemblance to the question of how long to set a traffic intersection light cycle. I think this is your answer." Ecco handed Austin a piece of paper and a brief proof.

"Thank you, Dr. Ecco," said Austin. "Now for the hard part. We want to reduce the pipe's capacity to 1.2 barrels per minute. We are willing to increase the size of one of the drums, but by as little as possible."

 (2) Which drum capacity should be increased and what should its new capacity be? How should the pipe then be used?

"Dr. Ecco, you certainly arrived at your conclusions quickly," said Austin after Ecco answered the second question. "I know many people who *could* use your services. If you want . . . . "

"Thank you, Ms. Austin, but no thank you." Ecco interrupted. "Professor Scarlet will tell you that I have refused most commissions from your industry. In some cases, your engineers would do a better job. In others your colleagues should hire soothsayers."

CHAPTER THREE

Experts

$$-\!(1)\!-$$

THE CAMPERS' PROBLEM

We must protect the truth with a bodyguard of lies.
—*Winston Churchill.*

If telling your friends when you are about to take an extended trip is a mark of loyalty, then Ecco is not at all loyal. He simply leaves word that he has gone. When he comes back, he just calls me up.

Most of his trips take him to unpeopled places along the ocean, most often on the Maine coast in the fall. "I eat some simple food, but mostly I walk. From time to time I lie down on the sand. The air is salty and misty. The seagulls never stop their high-pitched cries. It's the place where I collect my thoughts."

It was a few days after one such trip that one of the most challenging cases of Ecco's entire career came to his attention. We were playing a closely contested game of chess, although I could see trouble brewing as Ecco pressed his queen-side attack.

The phone rang and Ecco motioned for me to pick up the extension. "Dr. Ecco, we need your help," said the voice. "Uh . . . uh, Dr. Ecco, we detect a signal . . . someone is listening in."

Ecco smiled. "Yes, General. It is Professor Scarlet. Don't worry."

Ecco was less worried about surveillance now. The Director has assured him that the surveillance had ceased, but had asked him to restrict his travel plans to friendly countries.

"Oh, hello, Professor," said the general, "it's just that we must be careful. I will visit you in two hours."

"Agreed," said Ecco.

"Dr. Ecco, let me tell you a story," began the general when he arrived. Ecco smiled at me. The military often disguised their intentions in parables. It was either obvious what they were talking about or completely obscure.

"As I tell you the story, Dr. Ecco," the general continued, "please don't be misled by its innocent setting. We are dealing with important matters."

"Yes, General," said Ecco.

"Suppose, Dr. Ecco, that you were a camp counselor," said the General. "You and your eight campers are lost in the woods unable to find a path. Finally, you come to a four-way intersection of paths. You know your campsite is only 20 minutes away from there, but you don't know which path to take. You have an hour more of daylight, after which traveling is very dangerous. So you cannot travel with all eight campers down one route at a time. It would take too long.

"Instead, you must send small groups 20 minutes down each path and have them rendezvous at the intersection in 40 minutes. You will then decide which route to take. (You may also participate in the search in the first 40 minutes.)

Figure 4 After arriving at the crossroads, the campers have 1 hour to find and reach the campsite.

"The problem is that two of the campers in your group some-times lie. You do not know which ones they are. How do you divide up your group into search parties? At rendezvous time, how do you decide which way to go? You must be right no matter how the occasional liars — whoever they may be — are distributed among the groups and no matter whether they lie or not."

After the general finished, Ecco looked at me. "Professor, what do you make of it?"

"Well, there are nine people including the counselor and there are four possible paths," I replied. "Since the group has been in the wilderness, any path is possible. I think it would be useful if the counselor participated. Perhaps sending three peo-ple down each of three paths and having them come back after 20 minutes is a good idea."

"But suppose," said Ecco, "that two groups come back saying the campsite is not down their paths. Then suppose two campers from the third group say the campsite is down their path and one camper in the third group says it isn't. You wouldn't know whether the third path is the right one or the unexplored one is right. What makes the problem tricky is that liars may lie but need not."

"True," I admitted. "But still, three paths should be enough."

Ecco didn't answer. He was deep in thought. After some time, he smiled. "Professor, the counselor doesn't lie." A few minutes later he was explaining his answer to the general.

 (1) Try to solve the problem using Ecco's observation. (Solution on page 151.)

The general looked pleased with Ecco's solution, but he had more on his mind. "Dr. Ecco, it is possible that we will have only seven, er . . ., campers. Can you solve the problem then?"

 (2) Either give a method of solution or prove that no solution is possible with seven campers.

The general called a few days later asking for the solution of a much more difficult problem. "Dr. Ecco, suppose there could be five liars. How many campers would you absolutely need in that case to find the campsite and how would you do it?"

 (3) Try to show that whatever number you choose is the least possible. It should be under 20.

After Ecco had answered that one, he leaned back in his chair. "It all sounds like some communications problem to me, Scarlet. Transmitters fail on occasion, just as people lie on occasion, but perhaps they know that it is unlikely for more than two to fail around the same time."

"But what about the trusted counselor?" I asked.

"Yes, I must decide what his role might be," Ecco said. Before he could think about that, the phone rang. It was the general.

"Dr. Ecco," he said after introductions, "this may be the hardest problem of all. Suppose you have only four campers and the counselor, but still two of the campers sometimes lie. However, you have 100 minutes—time for two round trips—before the final decision is made. Is a solution even possible?"

 What do you think?

Ecco looked at me. "It seems tough," I said. "With four, there is no assurance that the truth tellers can outvote the liars. Then again, though, maybe we can make use of the fact that the campsite is down only one path."

"Very promising suggestion," Ecco said. He said it so fast that I could see he was already turning its implications over in his head. "General, we will think about it and call you back."

"Very well, Dr. Ecco," said the general. "But please hurry.

Also, it would help if you can spare some of the campers from making both trips."

Ecco began working right away. Three or four times he started off with great energy, then he would grunt and crumple up a piece of paper. I also worked at it, but without success. I saw him leaning back on his chair, staring at the ceiling. I stopped paying attention. Suddenly Ecco leaned forward in his chair and laughed.

"Why, professor, you have done it again," he said. "I can solve the problem. My reasoning depends on your excellent though enigmatic observations. You will note by the way that at least three of the four campers don't have to move the second round."

 (4) Solve the problem using four campers, two of whom sometimes lie. You have time for two exploratory trips and one final walk to the site. Note that each liar may lie when he or she pleases and how he or she pleases. For example, the liar may lie after the first trip and not the second, or vice versa.

"Your solution is so simple, yet so different from your previous ones," I marveled. "And yet you only use at most one camper in the second round. I can't help wondering whether three campers would be enough."

"Well," said Ecco, "if you knew that the two liars would always give the same answer if they went down the same path, you could certainly do it."

To this day, I still don't know how.

—②—
PEBBLES AND PERSUASION

It was a fetid, windless summer day in New York. Ecco was grumpy. "It's blowing 25 knots at Columbia Gorge and here am I in this steam bath. No clients, no windsurfing. I wonder what a Tlönist would do?"

Ecco often referred to the invented planet of Tlön, a creation of Jorge Luis Borges. In Tlön, objects have no continuous existence. Rather they multiply and disappear, simply by virtue of a person's concentration.

"Would I think myself into Columbia Gorge?" Ecco asked rhetorically. "Entering into the mind of the Tlönist, I might not. After all, going from discomfort to comfort so easily allows the possibility that I might be sent back just as easily. Even thinking of my sweltering apartment with the glee of someone who has just escaped would be enough to bring me back." Ecco continued nibbling on his crackers.

"Psychology is closer to mathematics than physics is," Ecco mused. "Physicists use math as a tool, as if it were some kind of wrench. But math is a figment of people's imaginations. Psychology, properly viewed, studies these figments."

The doorbell rang. The woman who entered walked with the confidence of a person in control of her surroundings. If the heat bothered her, she didn't show it.

"Which of you is Dr. Ecco?" she asked.

"At your service, Madam," said Ecco, straightening up in an effort to match the woman's poise.

"My name is Decker," she said, not wasting any time. "I'm an attorney and I have an extremely important case to summarize. The facts of the case are quite complicated, so the judge has allowed me to use five easels, each containing a roll of flip charts.

"I would like to present the argument so that whenever I show a new chart, all immediately supporting assertions and evidence are visible on the other easels. No chart should be presented twice. Also, each fact or assertion requires one chart.

"Let me give you a simple example. Suppose the facts A and B support assertion C, and fact D and assertion C support conclusion E. If I present those items in the order D A B C E, I need four easels. When I present C, all three of A, B, and D must be in view as well as C. However, if I use the ordering A B C D E, then I only need three easels. Once I present C, I can use the easels with A and B on them for other purposes."

"Sounds like a problem that professors solve when they use blackboard space," Ecco said, looking at me.

"Exactly," said the attorney. "I've tried to do this by using an auditorium blackboard. But the actual problem is tough."

Then she gave the relationships:

A, B, and C support M.
D and E support N.

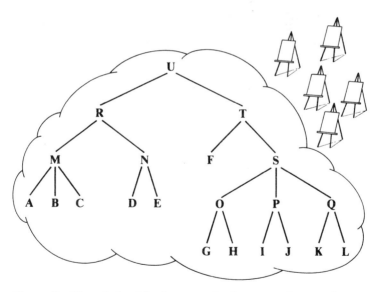

Figure 5 The relationships between the facts, assertions, and conclusions that Ms. Decker must show on her easels.

G and H support O.
I and J support P.
K and L support Q.
M and N support R.
O, P, and Q support S.
F and S support T.
R and T support U.

"I need to know whether I can present this case up to U with five easels, and if so, what charts should be on each easel and what order I should use. Remember that when a supported assertion is shown, all immediately supporting arguments must also be visible on the other easels. Remember also that each fact or assertion requires one chart."

Ecco began scratching on paper. I offered our guest some crackers, but she was intent on Ecco's doodling. After a few minutes, he began writing on a new sheet of paper.

"You certainly can do it," Ecco said.

 What is an easel layout and an order of presentation that supports Ecco's conclusion? (Solution on page 153.)

—③—
THE ARCHITECT'S PROBLEM

Most of Ecco's success as an omniheurist results from his ability to apply logic to problems that seem to fit into no special discipline. For example, no one has studied the mathematics of attorney summations. But Ecco's abilities stirred interest in the engineering design community as well.

After the great midwestern hotel disaster in which a structural defect and an underdesigned column caused many deaths in the early 1980s, many construction firms asked Ecco for his evaluation of their designs.

"I try to find contradictions in the designs; assumptions that a beam designer makes about vertical loads and supports that are not met by the designer of columns or space frames," Ecco once told me. "I don't try to find all of them. If I work long and hard enough and find none, they feel more confident. If I find any, they had better look for others."

"Can't you do better? Say, give them a guarantee of design correctness?" I asked.

"Sometimes I can," said Ecco. "But often anything approaching exhaustive testing is completely impractical. It is a fact of life: tests only reveal errors, they don't assure correctness."

Occasionally, designers have come to Ecco without a design to check, but rather with a set of constraints that they did not know how to meet. So it was with the well-known architect Emily Hayn. She was doing a project for a government Antarctic research team. "The problem, Dr. Ecco," she explained, "is bizarre. Most clients have ideas about layouts, but never so abstract or so seemingly impossible to satisfy.

"The instructions are to design a single story structure to contain 31 rooms, all of which are of 20 feet by 20 feet. (Let's ignore wall thicknesses; assume they have zero thickness.) Fifteen of the rooms have up to three doors. We are free to place the doors anywhere except the corners. The remaining 16 have only one door. One of the rooms also serves as the entrance to the structure (through one of its three doors). It must be possible to walk from any room to any other by passing through at most eight doors. There must be no hallways or any other structural features."

"So, no single-door room may have a door connected to another single-door room," Ecco pointed out with a chuckle. "Otherwise there would be no way to enter and leave those rooms."

"I was quite able to make that deduction, Dr. Ecco," said the architect, displeased with Ecco's light-hearted attitude. "If I cannot solve this problem by tomorrow, I will be out of a job. By the way, there is one more requirement: the structure is to fit on a plot of land 160 feet by 160 feet."

"But the problem really is not so difficult," said Ecco. With that, he wrote something very quickly and handed it to the young woman.

The paper that Ecco had given her was blank except for a capital letter H.

"But that's the source of the answer," protested Ecco, in response to her unspoken impatience. "I will produce the design for you in a moment."

 Try to think of your own design. (Solution on page 154.)

After the architect was satisfied that Ecco's design obeyed her specifications, she looked much more relaxed. "Sorry to have flared at you, Dr. Ecco," she said. "It's just that I thought you had given up — like everyone else I had asked — and were making light of my predicament."

"Not at all," said Ecco. "My apologies for being flippant. I wish you the best of luck with your project."

After the architect had gone, Ecco turned to me and smiled. "You've been thinking of the obvious question, too, haven't you, professor?" he asked.

"I think so," I answered. "Namely, does your solution require the fewest passages through doors possible?"

"Exactly," said Ecco. "The problem has quite a few points of interest. It is quite easy to show for starters that there can be only one way to get from any room to any other.

"The rest of the proof is much trickier and I shall have to think about it after a good chess game. What do you say?"

—④—
CIRCUITS CHECKING CIRCUITS

From time to time, I would drop by Ecco's apartment unannounced to discuss a mathematical problem or just to share tea and read. Ecco would open the door, motion me to a chair, and offer me tea, often without uttering more than a few words. This wasn't through any lack of friendliness (though Ecco's manner was anything but conventionally friendly), but because his readings and theorizing required long stretches of concentrated thought. Opening the door and sharing tea didn't disturb that concentration. Conversation certainly would have.

One such afternoon, I had tired of the paper I was reading. It had developed an extensive and complex notation and ended by proving little.

One of Ecco's notebooks entitled "Aesthetics in Math" was lying closed on his desk near me. I picked it up and opened it to the first page. It embodied an ideal that the paper I had been reading sorely lacked.

"Theories in the mathematical disciplines," it said, "don't have to fit facts. They need to have a simple elegance to them, though the elegance is seldom recognized unless the theory is somehow useful. Galois was a case in point. He developed group theory as a teenager in order to answer certain open questions of his day. At nineteen, still without having published anything, he died in a duel. Suspecting that he would lose, he spent the eve of his duel writing up his results. Frequently, he would interrupt a proof with the prophetic words *Je n'ai pas de temps* (I have no time). Galois' groups were accepted only decades after his premature death. It is hard to imagine modern mathematics without them. . . . "

It was then that a sharp knock at the door interrupted my reading. Ecco opened the door. The man in the blue suit introduced himself as Lars Pollard.

"My job is to design circuits that detect errors in other circuits," he said. "A primary control panel in a nuclear reactor sends out signals to 16 different motors. At any time, at most one motor should receive a 'go' signal. The others must receive a 'not go.' I must design a checking circuit to detect when two or more signals to the motors carry a 'go.' If so, the new circuit disables all the motors, which is always a safe thing to do."

"Circuit design is one of my favorite avocations," Ecco said, rubbing his hands in anticipation. "I assume the 'go' signal is transmitted as an electrically high signal (1), and 'not go' as an electrically low signal (0)."

"Precisely," responded Pollard. "We also have two kinds of components or gates to build with, called AND and OR. Both gates have at most eight input signals and one output. The output of the AND has the value 1 (electrically high) if all its inputs are 1; otherwise it has the value 0 (electrically low). The output of the OR has the value 1 (electrically high) if at least one of its inputs is 1; otherwise it has the value 0 (electrically low).

"For example, suppose there were only four signals, A, B, C, and D. Then we might put A and B into one AND, A and C into a second, A and D into a third, B and C into a fourth, B and D into a fifth, and C and D into a sixth. The outputs of all these would then go into a big OR gate. This would serve to detect multiple 'go' signals because if more than one signal were value 1, then one of the AND gates would have two imputs with value 1. Therefore that gate's output would have value 1, as would the OR gate. An output of value 1 tells us that more than one 'go' signal was received; an output of value 0 tells us that at most one 'go' signal could have been received.

"But using the method of comparing every possible pair for my original problem would require nearly 140 AND and OR gates. We would like to do it with one-tenth that many, namely 14. Also, each of the signals going to the motors may only be inputs to at most twenty gates of the checking circuit."

"A nice problem," Ecco agreed. "Would you be so good as to give me a day to think about it? I suspect that a new approach to the simple problem of four inputs might be promising."

When Dr. Pollard returned the next day, he found Ecco frowning as he read the chess column. "Even you had trouble with this one, didn't you, Dr. Ecco?" asked Pollard, depressed.

"Not with your problem, dear Dr. Pollard," said Ecco. "But with the chess game. How could white take black's pawn when the trap was so clear?"

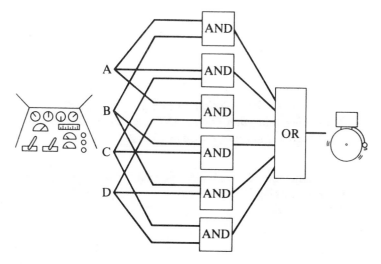

Figure 6 This circuit will successfully check four input signals. But Ecco doesn't think this is the right approach.

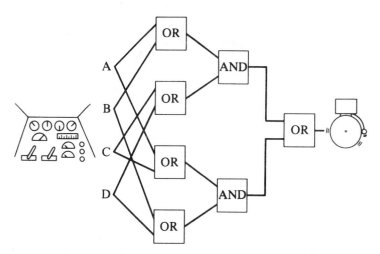

Figure 7 Another effective circuit with four input signals. If two or more input signals are 1, then the output is 1.

"So, you solved the problem?" asked Pollard.

"All except for one thing," Ecco teased as he handed Pollard a circuit diagram. "What are you going to do with the extra gate? Thirteen are quite sufficient to do the job you gave me."

 What is a 13-gate solution to Pollard's problem? Remember that each OR or AND gate may have up to eight inputs. (Solution on page 155.)

Ecco remembered the notebook that I had been reading. "Perhaps even Galois would have been pleased with this little solution," he said.

GOSSIPING DEFENDERS

People who renounce violence had better have strong friends.
  —*from Ecco's notebook, "Cynical Verities."*

Opening his apartment door to let me in one day, Ecco held a thick hardbound book in his left hand entitled *The Swiss Defense Strategy*.

He guessed my surprise and explained. "In a few minutes, Professor, we will be visited by one General Lange from the Swiss Army. As you know, Switzerland has not been in a war for several centuries. Part of the reason is that they always maintain a very strict neutrality in international affairs. Another is that they are anything but pacifists.

"They have mandatory military conscription and extremely tough training. Their mountains are their armories. Some say they even have airfields cut into mountains. Their soldiers are trained to fight in the mountains, in self-sufficient brigades. General Lange is responsible for communications within those brigades."

The general arrived a few minutes later. I couldn't help thinking that his physique embodied that rigorous training. He was rather short, but of muscular build and erect posture.

"Each of our brigades consists of 16 observation posts," he explained. "If an attack comes, each observation post would like to know the size of the enemy forces attacking every other post. Each post can determine the size of the enemy forces attacking it directly. So the problem is one of communicating the information. Each post can talk with another post in one minute. (The conversations are short, but the dialing and electronic counter-countermeasures take time.) If two posts talk, each one finds out everything the other one knows. How can we order the calls that each post makes, so that each post knows about the attacks on every other post in as few minutes as possible?"

"It is quite easy to do in four minutes," I said, explaining how.

 (1) How can the posts learn about all attacks in four minutes? (Solution on page 156.)

The general listened to my response as if he knew the answer. "Professor, we would like to reduce the necessary time to three minutes. Can we do that by reducing our defensive positions to 10 posts?"

"Certainly not," I said, backing up my assertion with an argument based on information exchange.

 (2) What is a convincing argument?

"I understand your reasoning, Professor," said the general. "One of our mathematicians has made an astounding claim.

Namely, with 10 defensive posts, communication will actually take five minutes instead of the four minutes it took with 16 posts. Is that possible?"

I must have looked confused, because the general's eyes quickly turned to Dr. Ecco, who looked pale. "It is getting late," he said. "Let us defer the question to after dinner, General, and you will have your answer at the end of the meal. I'll either give you a protocol such as the one the professor gave you or a proof showing that five minutes is necessary."

 (3) What must Ecco's answer have been?

"The remarkable thing about this problem is that in certain cases, it takes longer when there are fewer posts," mused Ecco after the general had left. "What is the simplest example you can think of, Professor?"

 (4) Try to find it.

—6—
DELICATE BALANCES

"Why do you think it is, Professor, that human beings have an almost universal desire to be designers?" Ecco asked rhetorically.

"Perhaps, you are overgeneralizing from your own inclinations," I answered.

"Perhaps," Ecco continued, "but consider this. Through most of human history, tradition and hard labor were far more important than design. Yet design must be basic to people's enjoyment of life just judging from its modern manifestations.

"We are overwhelmed with the results of design: advertisements, fad products, and fashion."

"But so many of these things are frivolous," I protested.

"True," said Ecco, "but think of the creative energy that goes into them."

"How are these speculations relevant to your researches?" I asked.

"Practically minded as usual, aren't you, Professor?" Ecco said. "Well, whether design is good or bad, it is certainly widespread."

"Agreed," I said.

"Well, whatever is widespread must have a natural explanation. Most biochemists think that creativity and the desire to design need not be explained by any cellular theory of the brain, but I disagree. The seed ought to be present even in the smallest neural cluster." Ecco sank into a reverie and began writing on his pad. He was still writing when the phone rang.

"Hello . . ." said Ecco. "Ah, Richard, how are you? Yes, we haven't seen each other since you were in architectural school. You've had quite a career . . . Oh, I have my sources. By all means, I would be happy to help you with your problem."

Richard Hackett arrived within the half hour. He was a tall, erect man wearing glasses, in his early thirties. In his left hand, he held a blueprint of the next space station. Ecco got up to greet him.

"The problem," said Hackett, "has to do with the weight of the connecting clamps. We must make sure they are as light as possible, because we must transport them all to space. Eighteen manufacturers have submitted samples of their clamps to us with 10 identical clamps per sample. We must determine which manufacturer's sample consists of the lightest clamps."

"You would hardly need my help to do that," said Ecco.

"Normally, I would agree. But for political reasons, the way I am supposed to determine which clamp is the lightest is by using the eight balances at the National Bureau of Standards. Each balance can compare two clamps at a time."

"So, you weigh manufacturer X's clamp against manufacturer Y's clamp in a balance. If the side with X's clamp goes down, then X is out. Is that right?" I asked.

"Exactly," said Hackett. "The trouble is, the Bureau will only allow my people to use their eight balances for 30 minutes. It takes 15 minutes to set up and clean the equipment. It then takes four minutes to balance two different clamps properly. So we only have time to do three sets of simultaneous balances with a minute in between to decide which balance should be used for which clamps in the next cycle. Can I do it and if so, how?"

 (1) What balancing strategy would you use to find the manufacturer that makes the lightest clamp? Remember that you have many copies of each clamp available. Also remember that you can weigh only one clamp against one other during a single balancing. (Solution on page 157.)

After Ecco had demonstrated his answer, Hackett became very thoughtful. "Well, then, could I compare clamps from more than 18 manufacturers in the same time?"

 (2) What is the maximum number of different manufacturers that can be handled in a half hour? Try to demonstrate your answer.

Hackett thanked us and Ecco escorted him to the door. "Good luck with your design, Richard," Ecco said warmly. "The next generation will look up to you as a pioneer."

CHAPTER FOUR

Polluters, Suitors, and Tigers

WAREHOUSES AND BARRELS

Ecco was in a teasing mood. "Universities thrive on complexity," he remarked. "But complexity is not the path to novelty, just to uniqueness. I'm not much of a student of business, but look at this article." He tossed a magazine clipping on the table in front of me.

The clipping read: "A man who started the wildly successful Fly-by-Night overnight mail delivery service proposed his ideas in an undergraduate term paper at Green College. He said the planes would fly to a central U.S. city, such as St. Louis. The packages would be transferred to other planes, and the original planes would return to their starting destinations with packages bound for those cities. His professor gave him a C. The young man just endowed the Fly-by-Night chair at Green."

Ecco watched as I put down the clipping. Then he said, "Yet the professor was justified by academic standards — the idea was uncomplicated, the student's thoughts were not deep. They were just good."

"So, the professor made a mistake," I conceded.

Ecco must have heard the edge in my voice. "Oh, excuse me," he said. "Perhaps it doesn't happen often, but you have to admit it's not all that surprising, is it?"

He shrugged and smiled. "Anyway, I bring it up because our client today has a kind of similar routing problem — but of toxic materials. I think you will like Mr. Barin of Universal Chemicals. He characterized his own job as manager of 'covert trucking.' I wonder what he means."

Shortly after our conversation, a heavyset but energetic gentleman was in the room explaining his problem. "We have eight warehouses with toxic chemicals," said Barin. "Each warehouse contains eight barrels, each filled with one kind of chemical. To avoid confusion, we call the chemicals c1, c2, c3, c4, c5, c6, c7, and c8, and the warehouses w1 through w8. Each chemical is not toxic by itself, only in combination with others. We want to organize the barrels so that all those containing chemical c1 are in warehouse w1, barrels of chemical c2 are in warehouse w2, and so on.

"We have decided to perform all the organizing moves by truck. Each truck can make one round trip between two warehouses in one day, carrying four barrels each way. For safety reasons and to avoid as much press attention as possible for a move of this kind, we don't want to use odd-looking trucks. Instead, we will use the most common kind of Mack truck, but with eight axles for stability and a reinforced compartment."

"Quite a coincidence of eights," said Ecco. "Let me make sure I understand correctly. There are eight different chemicals altogether. Each of your warehouses has one each of all eight. You want each warehouse to contain eight barrels of only one kind. Each truck in a given day can exchange only four barrels between two warehouses."

"Exactly," said Barin. "Now, we're considering having only one truck do all this moving, again for safety reasons, and to avoid publicity. In that case, what's the fastest method and how long would it take?"

 (1) What does Ecco answer? (Solution on page 157.)

But Barin was not satisfied. "That's a little too long," he said. "I'm sure the press would be on to us. What if we were willing to hire several trucks, but on the stipulation that only one truck can visit a given warehouse on any one day. That is, each warehouse can participate in only one exchange."

"Why, then it would take three days," said Ecco. "Here is the method."

 (2) Explain a method for accomplishing this.

"Are you sure you can't do even better, Dr. Ecco?" asked Barin.

"Quite sure," said Ecco. "If a warehouse can participate in only one exchange per day, then three days is as short a time as you can get."

 (3) Show that three days is as short a time as possible to accomplish the task.

PARTY

"Receiving a telegram these days is most unusual," Ecco said as he tore open the envelope. After reading the message, he said, "The contents are even more so. What do you make of it, Professor?"

The telegram read: DR ECCO NEED YOUR HELP ON RIDDLE STOP BELIEVE IT FROM GREEK MYTHOLOGY STOP WILL CALL ON YOU TOMORROW AFTERNOON END.

"You are something of an amateur scholar of Greek mythology, aren't you?" I asked, pointing to a row of books.

"Quite amateur, indeed," Ecco responded modestly, "but considering the tone of this telegram, possibly more knowledgeable than our client, who may even now be pressing the doorbell."

The young man at the door looked very athletic with his polo shirt and tanned face. After introductions, he explained his problem.

"The woman I love is a graduate student in Greek literature," he said. "Her latest eccentric demand is that I solve a riddle adapted from her researches. She will marry me if I can answer three questions. Will you listen?"

"By all means," said Ecco. "Please proceed."

"There is a party," said the young man, launching into the riddle. "Everybody at the party has shaken hands with three of the other people, except for one person, who has shaken hands with only one of the other people.

"That's all the information you get, Dr. Ecco." Then he stated the three questions.

1. What is the smallest number of people who could be at such a party?

2. Could there be 21 people at such a party?

3. Is there a general pattern of how many people could be at such a party?

 Can you answer the questions? (Solutions on page 159.)

It took Ecco nearly a day to answer the three questions. "The key thing," he concluded when he called the client into the room, "is to remember that hand shaking is symmetric. If X shakes the hand of Y, then Y shakes the hand of X."

The young man noted the answers, wrote Ecco a check, and left.

Ecco turned to me and said, "Why would the young woman lie to her friend about the riddle's origin? The questions, though difficult, are just not the right style for Greek mythology."

Ecco paused and fell into deep thought for several minutes. "Of course . . . the oracle at Delphi often posed questions that weren't supposed to be answered. Thinking about them helped the listener. Our young friend was meant to fail. In his attempt, he was to realize that he was not right for her. That was what these questions have to do with mythological riddles. Ah, Professor, have I done the wrong thing?"

"You have at least taught the young woman a lesson," I said. "Things have changed in the last three thousand years, and she should know that. The Greeks didn't have omniheurists for hire."

—③—
CODE BREAKING

Eccentrics, architects, lawyers, and spies have made up most of Ecco's clientele. On a splendid May day, a treasure hunter added himself to the list.

"A young man with a distinct West Virginian accent has called me up to ask for help," Ecco explained when I came over that day. "It seems that he is participating in a treasure hunt organized by a mail order house called, appropriately, It's Better to be Rich.

"I have obtained the brochure of these mail order people. It is a little vague on the nature of this treasure, but asks that the participants have faith. 'We ourselves did not become rich by accident,' says the brochure. 'We know what we are doing.'"

"That may well be," I said. "But does what they're doing benefit the treasure hunters?"

"Exactly the question," said Ecco. "I knew you were a good judge of human nature."

At that moment the doorbell rang. A man with a denim jacket, an open shirt, and well-worn pants entered. "Well, here I am. Jack Hanson is the name," he said extending his hand. "I sure hope you can help me, sir. I was the first one to reach the clue near the Hunt's Point market. It was in a back alley in the damndest neighborhood. I copied it down as accurately as I could, but I can't make anything of it. Do you think you can help? I really want to get this treasure. It's my one sure way of going back home to take my sweetheart away from her money-conscious daddy."

The young man handed Ecco the page. It read: xf kf jflkyvie fsjvimrkzfe nzeufn fw nficu kiruv tvekvi rk kve rd dfeurp dfiezex. rzd tvekvi kvcvjtfgv kfnriuj vcczj zjcreu. cffb wfi jrzcsfrk nzky sclv jrzc. wzerc dvjjrxv zj fe sreevi fw jrzcsfrk ze kyzj tfuv.

I looked at Ecco for his reaction. Maybe this was the same code, I thought, that has been used in the mysterious letters he's been getting.

"This may be long enough for you to break," I said.

Ecco studied the message for some time. "The first thing I will look for is a single substitution code (a code in which every letter of the encrypted message stands for a single letter in the original plain-text message) since those are the easiest to generate and the easiest to break. The word lengths are consistent with that hypothesis."

Hanson seemed very impatient. He paced around the room, picking up books and putting them down, all with exasperated sighs. Finally, he announced that he hadn't slept for days and he would return the next morning.

"Yes, come back about 11 A.M.," Ecco said to both of us as he began working. "I should have cracked the code by then."

I returned to Ecco's apartment at the appointed hour. Ecco's client was already there.

"You look like a man who likes heights and I hope you do, Mr. Hanson," Ecco said as he handed the decrypted message to our visitor. "I will see you in a day or two."

 (1) What is the message in decrypted form? (Solution on page 160.)

"Is this code relevant to the mysterious message we got from the Gorge?" I asked.

"No," Ecco replied. "Applying the new code to the other messages just yields rubbish. This one looks as if the contest makers are just having fun."

As Ecco predicted, Hanson returned the next day with a new sheet. This one just contained two words: slp zsd.

 (2) What is this message in decrypted form?

Ecco tried to suppress a chuckle as he handed Hanson the decrypted message. He knew it would not please the young man.

Hanson stood aghast. He began muttering loudly in a mostly unintelligible fashion, though I could hear the words 'crooks' and 'swindlers' quite distinctly. He paced around the room all the while. Ecco tried to comfort him.

"I'm sorry for the news, Mr. Hanson. But you never know. Maybe the treasure hunt designers have inside information."

CODE INVENTION

"Tell me, Professor," said Ecco as I entered one Wednesday at midday. "How familiar are you with Morse code?"

"Not very," I answered. "I once achieved the proficiency of five words per minute, but I never pursued it."

"Nor did I," said Ecco. "My apartment landlord would have looked unfavorably toward a ham radio antenna added to an already crowded roof. But I have had occasion to read about Samuel B. Morse himself. He was an Anglophile shortly after the American Revolution as well as a painter of considerable talent.

"And, of course, he was an inventor. He invented both the telegraph and the code. His initial intention was that the code would be used by governments to convey secret messages. Instead it became a communication medium of world use. Considering the identity of our next client, I have a feeling that we shall be truer to Morse's original vision."

We heard a knock on the door and the client stepped in. He was wearing a dark gray business suit with a white shirt and a burgundy tie. Conservative elegant stuff.

He didn't seem to like the looks of me. "Really, Dr. Ecco, I must ask to speak to you alone. These are matters of the greatest importance."

"Nonsense," said Ecco. "The professor is as upstanding a citizen as I. As for security, you weren't going to give me the contents of those seven code words you spoke of, now were you?"

"No," he admitted, "you are right. I suppose it doesn't matter."

"The situation is this," our still unintroduced client began. "There are seven code words, which we will call A, B, C, D, E, F, and G. These code words have different frequencies: A occurs on the average of 10 times out of 100; B, 20 out of 100; C, 9 out of 100; D, 31 out of 100; E, 7 out of 100; F, 4 out of 100; and G, 19 out of 100. All our messages are to be sent in dots and dashes, but unlike Morse code, which has pauses between letters, we want the code words to go out without pauses. We think it will be faster to send and harder for the enemy to understand.

"To guard against machine malfunction, these code words will be sent and received by human operators as well as by machine. Trained people can send dots accurately at the rate of two per second, including the silence before the next dot or dash. Dashes are slower, achieving rates of only one per second.

"Now, we have come to you, Dr. Ecco, to see if you can design a code for each of the seven code words such that the average message of 100 code words takes no more than 190 seconds to send and is unambiguous."

"What do you mean by unambiguous?" I asked.

Ecco smiled. "Suppose," he answered, "the code for E were dot and the code for F were dot dot; then two dots in a row could either be two E's or one F."

I nodded. The dots and dashes have to have a unique interpretation after all.

"We have come up with a code," Ecco's client continued, "but it doesn't achieve our goal. Frankly, I don't think it is possible. Let me explain my reasoning. Clearly, we want the D code word to be as short as possible because it occurs the most times, so we represent it just by dot. That means all the other six words must begin with dash, otherwise the dot could represent either the beginning of a word or a D. We make B be the next shortest, with dash dot. Continuing in this way, we make G, dash dash dot; A, dash dash dash dot; C, dash dash dash dash dot; E, dash dash dash dash dash dot, and F, dash dash dash dash dash dash dot. If 100 code words were sent, it would take 31 × 0.5 seconds for the D's, 20 × 1.5 for the B's, and so on. This gives (31 × 0.5) + (20 × 1.5) + (19 × 2.5) + (10 × 3.5) + (9 × 4.5) + (7 × 5.5) + (4 × 6.5). This totals 233 seconds."

Ecco turned to our guest. "Please be seated. A better solution should be possible, though D may have to take a bit longer. Professor Scarlet will excuse your initial distrust, I'm sure, if you play him a game of chess. In the meantime, I will work on your problem."

 Can you design a code meeting the specifications of Ecco's client? (Solution on page 160.)

When Ecco handed over the solution, the client nodded and smiled; it was the first good humor I had seen in him all day (I had thrashed him in our chess game). "Well, Dr. Ecco, you are worth your weight in code, if you will excuse the pun," he said.

"Just between us, do you think we are wise in requesting a code without pauses?" he asked, resuming his serious tone.

"Assuming you want the truth, sir," said Ecco, "no."

"Why not?"

"If your receiver should miss even a single dot," Ecco said, "the rest of the message will be completely misinterpreted. At least with pauses, the damage is limited to a single code word. Perhaps it can then be inferred from context."

The man was disappointed with this answer, but he didn't care to hear the remedy that Ecco must have had ready for him.

—⑤—
SPACECRAFT MALFUNCTION

Everyone different from me is a potential villain.
    —*from Ecco's notebook, "Sources of Prejudice."*

"It is said that court intrigues started with people lying about
other people, then lying about other people's lying, and so it
went, " Ecco told me when I visited him one day. "The intri-
guers constantly looked for a scapegoat who inevitably proved
to be someone with the least power, though not always the least
morality. Some scholars say that the main role of the court fool
was to expose these intrigues to the monarch.

"It seems that units in our space probes have their own
intrigues. When one unit malfunctions, some of the others are
supposed to accuse it of acting badly. If only one is so accused,
then it is probably bad. But if several are accused, then ground
control must determine which units are faulty. That, at least, is
all I know based on my phone conversation with Dr. Bugunter
who should arrive at any minute."

Dr. Bugunter was a fortyish man with coke-bottle-thick
glasses and a disheveled mustache. He had a mysterious air
about him. The existence of the space probe itself was a secret,
he told us. Its instruments were also classified, though the ones
that were causing problems had to do with flight control rather
than the actual experiment. (I beg the reader's indulgence for
having to protect some of the descriptive aspects of Ecco's
involvement with the Encounters Space Probe.)

"Units in our space vehicles are overdesigned because of our
concern about safety," Dr. Bugunter explained. "We want to
know when a unit is faulty, so various units check other ones.
Our spacecraft took off several days ago and some malfunctions
have occurred.

"The units are so reliable that it would surprise us very much if more than one were faulty. If more than two are faulty, we would lose the probe, so let's assume that at most two are faulty.

"Each unit checks at most two others. A good unit will give an accurate diagnosis of the units it checks. For example, if unit X is good and it says that Y is faulty and Z is good, then, in fact, Y is faulty and Z is good. However, a bad unit is unreliable. So, if unit X is faulty and makes the same statements, then Y may or may not be good and Z may or may not be good.

"We come to you, Dr. Ecco, to help us figure out which unit or units are faulty. Here are the claims made by each unit. In fault detection terminology, these claims are called the syndrome.

"A says that C is faulty; B says that A is faulty but C is good; C says that D is good but E is faulty; D says that F is good; E says that C is faulty but F is good; and F says that B is faulty.

"Now, Dr. Ecco, could only one unit be faulty? If so, which one?"

"No," Ecco said after a while, "more than one must be faulty."

 (1) How does Ecco know? (Solution on page 161.)

Dr. Bugunter was quite discouraged by this response. "Could two units be faulty, and if so which ones?" he asked.

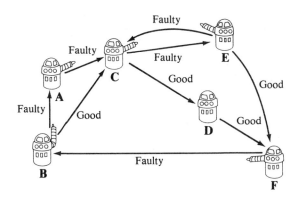

Figure 8   Spacecraft syndrome.

"Two units could explain your syndrome, Dr. Bugunter," said Ecco. "If two are faulty, they are . . . "

 (2) Which units are faulty? How do you know?

"Good," said Bugunter. "We will try shutting off those two. If that fails, I'll be looking for another job."

—6—

ESCAPED TIGER

I was going to a conference in India to present a paper. When I told Ecco, he offered to accompany me.

Ecco was only mildly interested in the conference itself, but he was very interested in the Taj Mahal in Agra, built 1632–54. "Few buildings in the world embody so much thought. As just a small example," he said, "the minarets are constructed at an angle so that if they were to fall, they would fall away from the magnificent central dome."

We arrived in New Delhi a few days before the conference began and Ecco set off immediately for Agra, though there were many worthwhile sites in the capital. He spent the days looking at "the Taj" from various angles and examining its inlays. He returned again and again to the riverside view (the back).

"The basic geometric abstraction is the circle," he explained to me when he returned to New Delhi. "This imposes a symmetry that should overpower the delicate beauty of the detailed marble workings, but for some reason it never does.

"Building the Taj was so expensive that when the Mogul emperor Shah Jahan made plans to construct a second mausoleum in black marble across the river, his son feared that the state would go bankrupt as a result. So the son put his father under palace arrest. Shah Jahan lived his last years with a view of the Taj Mahal and the knowledge that his black mausoleum would never be."

Ecco accompanied me during the first day of the conference. As usual, he attended under a false name, forbidding me to introduce him under any circumstances. Several papers referred to his work, although only about half did so for the right reasons ("defensive referencing," Ecco sniffed).

During the lunch break of the first day, we noticed a large crowd and many policemen outside. A high-ranking police officer entered our luncheon hall, stood on the podium, and addressed us as follows: "My name is Chief Inspector Singh. You have doubtless noticed the commotion outside your window. Let me explain. A tiger of the fiercest species on earth has escaped from a zoo and is hiding in an abandoned temple near here. The zoo only has three keepers who are trained to catch tigers. As you, ladies and gentlemen, are world-renowned mathematicians, perhaps you can tell us whether our three keepers can capture the tiger within three hours."

The inspector paused for a moment and then continued. "The tiger may be in any room. The tiger may run from one room to another while they are looking for it, although it won't run into a room that has a keeper in it.

"Now, let me tell you about the temple. It has no windows and only one entrance. Of its 19 rooms, 18 connect to either one other room or to three others. The 19th room connects to two other rooms. There are no doors of any kind between rooms. The rooms are dark and the tiger may find many hiding places, even though none of the rooms is very large. There is only one way to walk from any room to any other in the temple.

"We want to get the tiger out alive and uninjured, so we don't want to lay traps or put barriers between rooms. The temple is small enough so that moving from room to room takes almost no time. Doing a thorough search of a room takes a keeper 20 minutes. If he finds the tiger, he can use his stun gun. Time is of the essence, because the tiger can scratch its way through various parts of the temple walls in under three hours."

The room was immediately abuzz with activity.

"Do you know the layout of the temple?" asked one mathematician.

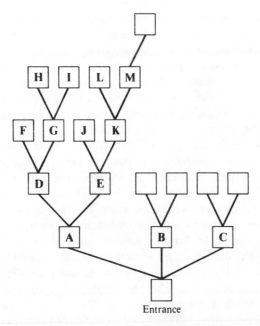

Figure 9 Inspector Singh's sketch of the connections among the rooms in the temple.

"Yes, sir, we do," said the chief inspector. "I will endeavor to draw it for you." The inspector drew a diagram with an entrance room, having three passageways to other rooms, which we will call A, B, and C. B and C each lead to two other rooms, all dead ends. A leads to two other rooms, D and E. D in turn leads to F, which is a dead end, and to G, which leads to H and I, which are both dead ends. E leads to J, which is a dead end, and to K. K leads to L, which is a dead end, and to M. M leads to another room that is a dead end.

"It is imperative, ladies and gentleman," said the inspector, "that at no time should the tiger have a free path to the entrance."

After a few minutes, Ecco walked to the side of the podium and handed the chief inspector a piece of paper. The inspector looked at it, huddling with Ecco over doubtful points, then shook his hand heartily and thanked him. Ecco then left the room.

"Thank you, ladies and gentleman, your colleague has solved the problem; it will take our men only about 2 hours and 20 minutes. He left the room before telling me his name. Good day to you all," said the inspector general.

 (1) How can the tiger be found so fast? (Solution on page 161.)

 (2) Is Ecco's time the best possible?

"What would you have done," I asked when I found Ecco again that evening, "if Inspector Singh hadn't been able to draw you a map? Suppose he had told you that the entrance connects to three other rooms; that there are 19 rooms in all; and that every room either connects to three others or to one other, with one exception that connects to two?"

"With just one way to go from any room to any other," Ecco added. "I'm certainly not sure I can do it as fast. Let's assume the tiger can't escape by scratching through the walls."

 (3) Can you suggest a plan to the three keepers that will allow them to eventually catch the tiger given any arrangement satisfying these conditions?

On our way home, Ecco and I couldn't find two seats together. So Ecco sat next to a young man in a business suit. I overheard Ecco say, in response to the man's questions, that he had been in India as a tourist. When Ecco returned the question, the young man simply said, "Oh, just visiting."

Hours later, I was roused by Ecco's rough shaking of my shoulder. "We must exchange seats," he said. "This man wants something from me."

"What do you mean?" I asked. "How do you know?"

"He started asking me about combinatorics, then about catastrophe theory. I hadn't told him my name, but I'm sure he knew.

Just as my suspicions were at their height, he asked me, 'Who do you think broke into your apartment when you went to the Gorge, Dr. Jacob Ecco?'"

I shook my head to make sure I wasn't dreaming. Ecco just nodded. "Scarlet, I asked him who he was and he just smiled. 'You will know when I want you to.' He then fell silent."

I exchanged seats with Ecco, but the young man looked sound asleep. When we landed, he quickly disappeared into the crowd. It was only when I unpacked that I discovered a strange envelope in my bag. In it, there was a new message: ow fwwv qgmj zwdh, sdgfw.

CHAPTER FIVE

Industrialists and Generals

$$\overset{\textstyle\frown}{-1}-$$

SPECULATIONS

We all remember that time as "the year of insanity." Prices went up, then down, then up, then down again. The markets, particularly for precious metals, fluctuated so wildly that the government finally intervened to try to calm things down. Their efforts were to no avail until, over a period of a several weeks, the markets seemed to calm themselves.

How Mark Stanley helped resolve this crisis has only begun to be whispered about. It is said that he prospered and simultaneously brought order to the market. His genius as an optioneer is common knowledge.

What is unknown is that Stanley had help. The reader might have already guessed the name of his helper.

In his dark suit, white shirt, and conservative tie, Stanley looked every bit the Wall Street figure when he entered Ecco's apartment that cold March day. He looked at us a bit skeptically, I must admit.

"Dr. Ecco," he said, "we have a serious problem in the markets as you know. We have tried all normal methods and they have failed. You are the last hope before the crystal ball gazers. Maybe nothing will work."

"Many have come to me without hope," Ecco responded cheerfully. "Please state your problem."

"Very well," said Stanley. "Because of the wild speculations in the gold market, the government has stepped in to try to keep things in order. Their policy is to set the price of gold for a given day by buying or selling gold at that price as the market demands. If the government sells more on a given day than it buys, it raises the price by a dollar on the next day. If the government supply increases, it lowers the price the next day. In the rare case that the supply stays virtually the same, the government doesn't change the price at all.

"For example, if the price on a given day is 600 dollars per ounce, on the next day it would be either 599 dollars (supply had increased), 600 dollars (supply had stayed the same), or 601 dollars (supply had dwindled).

"Whereas the government regulates the actual supply in this way, the prices are still fluctuating over the weeks, largely because of the activities of individuals known as optioneers.

"Optioneers sell people what comes down to a bet on the price of gold. A 'call' is a bet that the price will go up. A 'put' is a bet that the price will go down. If you buy a call from an optioneer and the price goes up a dollar per ounce, the optioneer gives you a dollar. If it stays the same or goes down, the optioneer gives you nothing. In either case, your option expires. A put is just the opposite. If you buy a put and the price goes down a dollar, the optioneer gives you a dollar. If the price stays the same or goes up, the optioneer gives you nothing."

"How much does one have to pay for one of these one-day bets?" I asked.

"Exactly the question I want to ask you and Dr. Ecco," said Stanley.

"Well, it better be less than a dollar," I observed.

 (1) How does the professor know that? (Solution on page 163.)

Ecco and Stanley both smiled in agreement. "Yes, Professor," said Stanley, "you survive your first lesson. But now the hard part. You see these optioneers get hunches. Especially toward the end of the day.

"For example, one optioneer named Noriaty is charging 60 cents today for a call but only 30 cents for a put. Noriaty has caused a lot of havoc in the market. So far, he has been the only optioneer. His strange hunches and stranger prices have aggravated the fluctuations. People figure he knows what he is doing, so they are willing to buy his more expensive options, almost no matter how he prices them. The only good thing about him is that he will always sell a customer as many options as the customer wants at the same price.

"I would like to establish myself as a strong competitor in order to make the options markets more rational. I won't hide my intentions from you either, gentlemen. I want to become rich."

"How unusual," said Ecco smiling. "Tell me, Mr. Stanley, you can buy gold yourself, correct?"

"And sell it, too," responded our visitor.

"You are also allowed to sell options aren't you?" Ecco continued.

"Yes, I finally have enough capital," said Stanley.

"Well then, you can earn quite a lot of money today by selling as many calls as you can at 55 cents."

"But the price may go up and then I lose 45 cents per call," said Stanley. "Noriaty is almost never wrong in his pricings."

"Oh, we can eliminate the risk by suitable interactions with Mr. Noriaty and the government," Ecco said assuringly. "Here is a strategy that you can follow to guarantee yourself a profit on every call option you sell."

 (2) What is Ecco's strategy?

"That's remarkable," said our visitor. "You have shown that the likelihood that gold will go up or down is irrelevant to the price of the options. It is all very logical, but it is so counterintuitive."

"Not only that," said Ecco, "but should Noriaty ever make the puts cost more than the calls, you can earn the difference again."

 (3) Describe a strategy if Noriaty prices the puts at 60 cents and the calls at 30 cents.

A few days later, Mark Stanley came back a richer and more confident man. "Dr. Ecco," he said, "Noriaty lost a bundle to me the other day. So much that he raised the price of both his calls and his puts to 60 cents. Remarkably, people are still flocking to him."

"Well then, sell as many of both in equal numbers as you can for, say, 55 cents," I suggested.

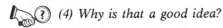 *(4) Why is that a good idea?*

Stanley took my advice and completely undercut Noriaty. Stanley not only became an overnight multimillionaire, but he also established himself as a center for options activity. The newspapers began referring to him as "the Noriaty stalker."

About a month passed before Stanley returned. Ecco seemed to expect him.

"I'm not surprised you're here, Mr. Stanley," said Ecco pointing toward the newspaper.

Stanley smiled nervously. He had taken to smoking even as he accumulated his millions. He seemed convinced that it would all end in ruin soon enough.

"So, you've seen it," said Stanley with a sigh. "The government is planning to change the price by two dollars a day instead of one in an effort to follow long-term trends better. Judging by our experience, the price will probably go up or down nine out of ten days, staying the same only one out of ten days.

"Noriaty vows to hold the line at a 60-cent option, just daring me to raise my prices. That will let him back into the market. So far, my strategy has been to sell as many puts as calls. Can I keep that strategy? What should I do?"

"Take a vacation," said Ecco. "Noriaty won't last long, I assure you."

 (5) How does Ecco know?

"But I don't want to go out of business," said Stanley. "What should my prices be in order to be safe but still be in the running?"

 (6) What did Ecco say? (The price you quote must be safe no matter how frequently the price stays the same from day-to-day.)

Noriaty did indeed go out of business. Once Stanley understood Ecco's reasoning, he became one of Noriaty's best customers.

RAILROAD BLUES

It was a gusty day in February, but our visitor wore only a light sweater. His face was weathered, perhaps the result of many winter fishing trips on iced-over lakes. Speculations aside, the man was from Wisconsin, the chief engineer of a small but thriving steel mill. His name was Hank Duffy.

His problem, he explained, had to do with getting iron ore from a mine to the mill, which was 100 miles away. The company had a one-track railroad and a single train. The train went back and forth as often as possible.

"We carry the iron ore as pellets in a train consisting of a locomotive in front, a caboose in the back, and 18 freight cars in between.

"Every day, we try to make as many shipments as possible from one end to the other, since our plant is running at full capacity. In fact we just got the last eight cars recently in order to prepare for a new plant that we have just built. Dr. Ecco, we

will need all the capacity we can get once we get that new plant
going. So, we've got to figure out how to turn the longer train
around in a short time.

"Let me give you a few more details. Each car can couple
with other cars on either side. When making the 100-mile trip,
the locomotive should be in front and the caboose should be at
the rear. The freight cars can be in any order. But for the purpose
of turning around, the locomotive can back up and can be in the
middle of several cars. The caboose can also be between freight
cars, but only the locomotive has power.

"Near each end of the track, we have a siding that can fit 13
of the cars. Beyond the siding, there is room for another 30 cars.
I'm sure you can figure out how we used the siding when we had
only 10 freight cars."

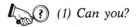 (1) Can you?

"Well," I said, "it's really quite easy. Drive the entire train
into the siding. Then drive backward out of the siding, throw the
switch, and return in the other direction."

"Right," said our visitor.

"You missed your calling as a trainyard engineer, Professor,"
Ecco said with a smile.

I wasn't sure I was flattered, but the next problem proved to
be a lot tougher in any case.

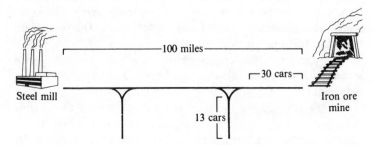

Figure 10 A single track with sidings on both ends connects the
steel mill to the iron ore mine (not to scale).

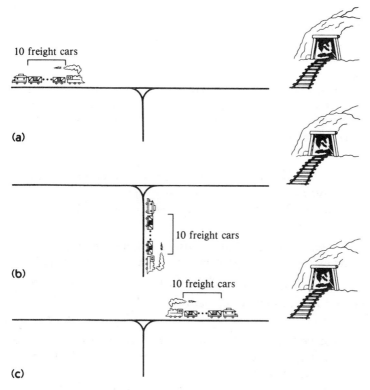

Figure 11 With 10 freight cars, the train can reverse direction easily. (a) The train is coming toward the mine. (b) The train goes down the siding. The locomotive can now push the train out. (c) The train is ready to travel toward the steel mill.

"For a train with 18 freight cars, the siding isn't long enough," said Duffy. "We have to uncouple — that is, disconnect — parts of the train, use the siding somehow, reconnect the train, and head off in the opposite direction.

"What takes time is those couplings and uncouplings. Uncoupling one part of a train from another takes two minutes. Coupling two cars takes about five minutes. Moving the train a few car lengths doesn't take much time at all. It's really the couplings and uncouplings. We have not been able to turn a train around in fewer than three couplings and uncouplings.

"Can you, Dr. Ecco, tell us how to do it in less time than that or can you prove that it can't be done in less time?"

Ecco thought about this for some time in silence. "You say, Mr. Duffy, that while turning around the train, it is all right for the locomotive to go backward?"

"Yes, that's right," said our visitor. "You can even have it push the train or part of it. Remember that it can couple in front or back as can any other car, including the caboose. But again, only the locomotive has any power."

 (2) Can you show how to turn the train around with at most two couplings and two uncouplings? Or can it not be done? (Solution on page 164.)

"I see, yes, I see," said our visitor. "You have saved us a lot of time. Tell me, can you show that you can't do better?"

 (3) Is it possible to do better?

"You've been very helpful, Dr. Ecco. If you ever have need for titanium-reinforced steel, you can be sure you'll get a good price," said Duffy.

"I have little room for construction equipment in my apartment, Mr. Duffy," Ecco said with a chuckle. "But next time someone asks me to consult on bridge design, I'll ask them to make a study of your steel."

—③—
FLIGHTY IDEAS

For me, this supersecret affair started when I arrived at Ecco's apartment one Saturday morning. Evangeline opened the door. She was about to recount a startling story of academic brutality perpetrated by the brilliant, though misguided, logician Benjamin Baskerhound.

"A world-famous linguist came to Princeton to give a talk entitled 'Why Are There No Double-Positives?'" Evangeline began. "He started by introducing the double-negative. He gave examples like 'I cannot afford not to do X,' which means 'I must do X.' He explained that the double-negative yields a positive. People in the audience nodded to indicate understanding.

"The speaker then presented his thesis: 'No one has recorded a double-positive as meaning anything in any language.'

"As soon as the speaker said this, Baskerhound cracked his pencil. It seemed to be deliberate. He looked straight at the lecturer and said in a high-low sing-song, 'Yea, yea.' After a moment of shock, the audience broke out into chuckles. The linguist turned pale and seemed about to faint."

I laughed, but Ecco sighed. "Reminds you of something, eh, Professor?" he said turning to me. "I wish I had been that witty. But then again, it is such a mean thing to do."

I explained to Evangeline how I had first seen the adult Ecco doing something very similar to a young topologist. Evangeline said, "Yes, Jacob seemed to feel very bad about that incident."

"By the way," I asked, "how did you two meet?"

"Always the inquisitive biographer, aren't you, Professor?" said Ecco. "Well, I'll tell you. While still at Oxford, Evangeline wrote a paper entitled 'Why We Can't Be Sure About What We Know So Far.'

"She showed that knowledge logics were flawed in their assumption of unchanging world axioms. She then presented a method to perform inference when inconsistent axioms are introduced into a world theory."

Evangeline continued the story. "Jacob wrote me a letter requesting to be put on my mailing list. He also asked me not to divulge his address to anyone else. Now, you must understand that Jacob's whereabouts were still the gossip mystery of young mathematicians and theoretical philosophers. I eagerly sent some papers and requested some from him.

"He sent me back three. They were written by the same author, but his name was not Jacob Ecco. He asked me not to divulge his pseudonym either. I sent him some questions about the contents of the papers."

Ecco picked up his side of the story. "Anyone who could ask such insightful questions was worth more than a scholarly correspondence. So I asked Evangeline out to lunch. We stayed until the restaurant closed that night and—"

A sharp knock interrupted Ecco. I opened the door and three men entered, nearly pushing me aside. They were dressed in U.S. Air Force uniforms. Their leader did not wait for introductions.

"Dr. Ecco, please excuse the interruption, but we have a problem of major importance," he said. "Who are your friends?"

Ecco introduced us and said, "General Evans, please state your problem when you are calm."

"Our squadron supports intelligence offices in eight East Coast cities and eight West Coast cities," Evans began. "We also have 16 planes. Every day we send packages from the West Coast cities to the East Coast ones. We formerly used a hub system. One plane would fly from each West Coast city to the hub city, say, Denver. The crews would exchange packages, so that each plane would then fly on to an East Coast city with just the packages for that city."

"Unfortunately, security considerations now dictate that no more than two of our planes should be in any single city over the course of a day. This obviously rules out the possibility of having a hub city.

"We would like to start off with two planes from each West Coast city and have each plane fly to a few airports on the way to the East Coast, exchanging packages at each airport. At the end of the trip we want any package from any West Coast city to arrive at whatever East Coast city it is addressed to.

"Speed is still critical. We find that the important limit to speed is the number of stops each plane makes. If you've been around airports lately, you know why.

"Can you find a strategy that delivers packages correctly, with each plane making only two intermediate stops—three landings in all? Remember that only two planes may fly to any city, including any destination city."

"How many airports are available for landing?" asked Ecco.

"Oh, many," said our visitor, "at least 30. But remember, each plane can only make three stops in all."

"What is the capacity of the airplanes?" Ecco asked.

"Ample," said our visitor. "If there were time, all the packages could be carried by one airplane."

Ecco looked at Evangeline and me. Evangeline was drawing on paper. Then he looked at our guest. "I'm afraid this will take me some time to figure out," he said. "Would you be so kind as to return tomorrow."

Our guest shook his head. "We must have the answer now," he said.

Now Ecco shook his head. "But it is not that easy," he muttered.

"Nor so hard, Jacob," said Evangeline, handing our guest a diagram. "I think this will satisfy you, sir."

 What is the answer? Show either that it can or cannot be done. (Solution on page 166.)

Our guest studied the diagram carefully. "It works, thanks very much, Miss, er . . ." said the man.

"Dr. Goode," Ecco said smiling.

"Ah, yes, Dr. Evangeline Goode, from Montana I believe. Rhodes scholar and logician," the officer said, extending his hand. "It is a pleasure to meet you. Thank you for your help. Please be so good as to forget my visit to you today. Good day, gentlemen, Dr. Goode."

Permission to publish this puzzle was granted only after the strategy was described in *Aviation Week*.

THE ROTARY PROBLEM

Mr. Silkman introduced himself as a traffic engineer. He began his explanation from the basics. "A rotary," he said, "is a circu-

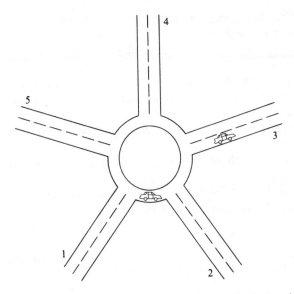

Figure 12   A five-way rotary. Cars move counterclockwise around the rotary.

lar road with several entrances and exits. It works as follows: a car enters the rotary, goes counterclockwise as far as it needs to and then leaves. For example a five-way rotary looks like this. A car entering road 1 must pass one entrance (road 2) to exit at road 3. To exit at road 5, the car must pass three entrances (roads 2, 3, and 4).

"The advantage of a rotary over traffic lights is that in light traffic no car is delayed. The disadvantage is that there tend to be more accidents. The number that reflects this tendency toward accidents is called the *danger number*. The danger number of a car on a single rotary is the number of merges it must perform both to enter and to drive on that rotary. That is, the danger number is the number of entrances that the car passes on the rotary plus one (for the entering merge). The danger number would be 2 for a car entering at road 1 and exiting at road 3, and it would be 4 for a car entering at road 1 and leaving at road 5. We don't count the exit since no merging is required there.

"Now, we have a problem that is unheard of in traffic history. We must design an intersection for 12 two-way roads. We wanted to use overpasses and switchbacks, but they are too expensive. We thought of one big rotary, but then an entering car may have a danger number of 11 in order to enter from a road and to exit from the road immediately clockwise from it. If the car wants to make an effective U turn, it would have a danger number of 12."

"So, one option," I said, "might be to have two rotaries each with six roads on them in addition to a road linking the two of them. An effective U turn would then only have a total danger number of 7, but there are certain other routes with total danger numbers of 12."

"That's right," said Silkman, "but rotaries still seem to be the only available option. Can you design a system of rotaries (the rotaries may be connected to each other by intermediate roads) such that every car has a danger number of less than 10 no matter where it wants to go, including an effective U turn?"

 How do you answer? If yes, show your rotary design. If no, prove your result. (Solution on page 167.)

"Is that the best you can do, Dr. Ecco?"

Ecco thought about this for some time. I had to leave before hearing his answer, however.

THE CONTRACT PROBLEM

"Consider the problem of signing a contract," Ecco said to me abruptly as we were drinking tea following our chess game one Saturday.

"What problem?" I asked. "Surely, the signing is not the tough part. The negotiations have come to a successful conclusion. The parties agree on all the points. What remaining problem should signing cause?"

"So you would think," Ecco replied. "But imagine the advantage if you could have only the other person sign. Consider an order for a commodity or stock. Suppose you put in an order to buy gold, but you didn't sign the contract. The seller does. If the price goes up, you acknowledge the contract. If the price goes down, you never signed it. At least, that's the ploy Ariana Radan suggested over the phone."

Within a half hour, Ariana Radan entered Ecco's apartment. For a lawyer, she seemed to know a lot about codes.

"In order for you to help me, gentlemen, you must understand one of the most elegant ideas of the computer age," she said. "A public-key encryption system works as follows. There are large number of pairs of mathematical functions. Each pair consists of an encoding function E, and a decoding function D. If m is a message in plain text—that is, one that anyone can read and understand—then $E(m)$ is an encoding of m and is unreadable. $D(E(m))$ is the decoding of the encoding of m. That is, $D(E(m)) = m$. Similarly, $D(m)$, the decoding of m, is unreadable, but the encoding of the decoding of m, $E(D(m)) = m$. The first critical property is that if m and m' are different, then $D(m)$ and $D(m')$ will differ as will $E(m)$ and $E(m')$. The likelihood that they won't is less than the likelihood that you're dreaming my visit. The second critical property is that knowing D doesn't help you determine E, or vice versa."

"Except for the last point, this doesn't seem so different from a classical system," said Ecco.

"Oh, but there is all the difference in the world," said Radan. "Suppose person X wants to send a message to person Y. In a classical system, X and Y would both know the method of encoding and decoding. Then X encodes the message and Y decodes it. The trouble is that X and Y must share their code, and this could fall into unfriendly hands."

"True," said Ecco. "Or these 'unfriendly hands' could decipher the code, as we have had occasion to do, right, Professor?"

I nodded and smiled, remembering well our hapless treasure hunter.

"Did I understand correctly, Attorney Radan," Ecco continued, "that the decoding function cannot be figured out from the encoding function or vice versa, and that there is no other way to decipher the encrypted code?"

"Exactly," said Radan. "In a public-key system, the encoding functions E_1, E_2, and so on are public knowledge. Only the decoding functions are secret. Breaking the code or even determining the decoding function corresponding to an encoding function is virtually impossible, as you have guessed. Not only for people, but even for the most powerful computer imaginable.

"Here's how a public-key system is used. If Y is the only person holding the decryption function D_y, X may send $E_y(m)$ to Y over public lines, which anyone can tap, but only Y will understand it by applying $D_y(E_y(m)) = m$.

"The system also allows the message to contain a kind of signature," Radan noted. "For example, if X is the only one holding D_x, then X can send $E_y(D_x(m))$. Person Y in turn retrieves the message by applying D_y and then E_x. Since only X holds D_x, Y knows and can prove that the message had to come from X. Such a protocol consisting of encoding and decoding functions should be the solution to our problem."

"Please proceed," said Ecco.

"Amalgamated Inc. and Behemoth Ltd. have just orally agreed to sign an indefinitely long series of contracts corresponding to stock purchases," Radan continued. "They would like to sign them electronically.

"If they trusted each other, Amalgamated could use its decoding function D_a, followed by Behemoth's encoding function E_b to encrypt the plain text, (that is, the contract). D_a acts as the signature of Amalgamated. Similarly, Behemoth could use D_b and E_a.

"The trouble is that neither company trusts the other that much. Amalgamated thinks that Behemoth will neglect to sign one contract at the last minute while holding onto the electronic copy that Amalgamated has signed. Behemoth has a similarly low opinion of Amalgamated.

"They have hired us to act as a judge. These are the requirements they have set upon us.

"First, assume that each company has kept its decoding key secret and has published its encoding key. Second, assume that each has a copy of the plain text of each contract they plan to sign. Third, for any given contract, assume that at least one of the companies obeys whatever protocol we set up. To certify the exchange our protocol must ensure the following:

1. We (the lawyers) must verify that the message each of them sends comes from the same plain text for each contract in the series.

2. We are not to see this plain text in unencoded form.

3. We must verify that each message contains the appropriate signature.

4. We must verify that the only people who can decode to plain text are those who know either D_a or D_b.

5. Neither company can obtain a signed contract by cheating.

"Dr. Ecco, we need your help in designing a set of encodings and decodings that each company should issue and a further set that we ourselves should use to help us solve this problem."

Ecco thought for a moment. "You have an encryption pair, I presume?" he asked.

"Yes, certainly," said our visitor, "they are D_z and E_z."

"Well, then I think it can be done, though it's tricky," said Ecco.

 What is a protocol that works? It should contain the functions that each company applies to the text it sends and what additional functions the lawyer's firm should use. Remember that for any message m *and for any decoding/encoding pair D_3 and E_3, $D_3 (E_3(m)) = m$. You may assume that for any message m, and for any decoding or encoding functions f1 and f2, f1 (f2(m)) = f2(f1(m)). (Solution on page 167.)*

Radan stood by nervously watching Ecco write, bite his pencil tip, shake his head, and write some more. "Do you think he can really do it?" she whispered to me more than once.

"I've never seen him fail," I said.

Finally, Ecco finished. "Attorney Radan, I may be wrong, but I think my solution is the simplest one possible under the circumstances. See what you think."

After reviewing the protocol, Radan looked very pleased. "You came highly recommended, Dr. Ecco," she said, "only the recommendation understated your talents."

Ecco bowed slightly to acknowledge the praise. Ariana Radan left.

$$-\!\!\!\underbrace{6}\!\!\!-$$

COMMAND AND CONTROL

"You will be pleased to know, dear Professor, that Herr General Lange will soon pay us another visit. He gave me only the roughest sketch of his problem. Let me fill you in before he comes.

"General Lange is now in charge of communication among the command and control centers. These units therefore put their members at high risk. That is all he told me over the telephone."

General Lange was wearing a newer and more ornate uniform. He had been promoted to a higher rank after resolving (with Ecco's appreciable help, if you recall) the problem of the gossiping defenders.

"This is a down payment," he said chuckling. He brought out a package that contained a wide variety of Swiss chocolates.

After telling us about the responsibilities of his new position as officer in charge of command and control, he began describing the problem.

"We in Switzerland," he said, "believe in simple technology. With the modern sensors that the superpowers and others are inventing, only shielded cables are safe from electronic eavesdropping. The trouble is that the safest connections are one-way and point-to-point (one sender and one receiver), but these are inconvenient as you will observe.

"We have divided each region into 15 command and control centers, a commanding one and 14 subordinate ones," he said. "From time to time, the commander may want to send messages to his subordinates and the subordinates may want to send messages to the commander. It is very important that these messages cannot be intercepted by the enemy. That's why our communication units are shielded.

"Each unit consists of a transmitter connected by a long wire to a receiver. The transmitter can only send and the receiver can only receive. The wire can be as long as we wish. Each control station (including the commander) gets the transmitters of two units and the receivers of two other units. Thus, each control station can be connected by one-way communication to up to four other control stations. Altogether there are 30 communication units.

"It takes about a minute for a station to send a message on a transmitter. The sender may, however, send a message to two stations at the same time, using his two transmitters. The receiver of a message can pass it on in another minute.

"We want the control stations to be connected so that as long as none are incapacitated, the commander can reach any other control station within three minutes and each control station can reach the commanding control station in four minutes. It is possible that the same message may reach its destination through different intermediaries and at various times."

"If all you required were that the commander could reach each subordinate in three minutes, you could do it with 14 units and no one would have more than two transmitters or two receivers," I observed.

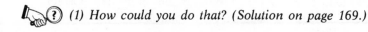 *(1) How could you do that? (Solution on page 169.)*

"That's true, but we are very concerned that the subordinates can send messages to the commander," said the general, "so that is a firm requirement.

"There is actually one more requirement and this is the trickiest. A control station may be incapacitated and be unable to send or receive any message. They will be well hidden, so we don't expect more than one to be hurt during the battles. In that case, we want the commander to be able to send a message to any subordinate within four minutes and receive a message from any unhurt subordinate in five minutes. In those situations, subordinates may have to communicate with one another without counting on the commander. So, if any control station is incapacitated (including the commanding one), any control station should be able to send a message to all functioning control stations within eight minutes. Can you do this, Dr. Ecco, with 30 transmitter/receiver pairs?"

Ecco had to think about this for some time, but he finally gave the general a connection pattern that worked. I was pleased to see that it included my connections as a subset.

 (2) Can you find a connection pattern that works?

"Tell me, Ecco, is it possible to do this with any fewer than 30 units?"

 (3) What is Ecco's answer and how does he prove it?

"General," Ecco suggested, "shall we go out for dinner so we can come home to enjoy these chocolates as dessert?"
"*Eine ausgezeichnete Idee,*" the general replied.

WRONG NUMBER

"Have you heard of the 'switch bug'?" Ecco asked as I entered one day.

"Yes, I think I have," I said. "Ultimate Switch, a major manufacturer of telephone switches, has made a design error, so that periodically the switch seems to transpose two neighboring digits among the last five. As a result, a person who dials 12345 as the last five digits might be connected to a number whose last five digits are 21345, 13245, 12435, or 12354. It has caused so many complaints that the media has given it the name of 'switch bug'."

"That's right," said Ecco. "Now the telephone companies are

wondering what to do with all the customer complaints. They have engaged my fellow graduate student Pauline Mingham to help them. Here she is now, I think.''

Dr. Pauline Mingham's name was well known to me. Her expertise lay in information theory, that branch of communications concerned with transmitting signals in noisy environments. Her papers had been widely published.

"We are willing to ask people to dial six digits instead of five if that would make the great majority of transposed numbers reach a nonfunctioning number.''

"Let me make sure I understand you correctly,'' Ecco said. "If there were only 10 people and you wanted a two-digit system, I could suggest 01, 12, 23, 34, 45, 56, 67, 78, 89, 90, right?''

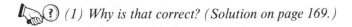 *(1) Why is that correct? (Solution on page 169.)*

"Yes, that's one approach that would work,'' said Mingham. "To get from any functioning number to another one requires dialing two numbers differently. So any number that is transposed would reach a nonfunctioning number.''

"In that case, I can solve your problem with six digits. Here's how,'' said Ecco as he laid out his solution.

(2) Given 100,000 five-digit numbers, find a set of 100,000 six-digit phone numbers such that a transposition between any two neighboring digits yields a nonfunctioning number. If possible, the only change should be that a sixth number is added to each existing number.

"An elegant solution,'' said Dr. Mingham. "I will arrange that you get the credit you deserve, Jacob.''

"Oh, not that, Pauline, please," said Ecco. "It was a charming problem, but I abhor publicity."

She nodded agreement and turned to leave, but Ecco said, "Pauline, don't go. Evangeline, Professor Scarlet, and I are going to the Blue Note jazz club to hear Herbie Hancock. I have reservations. Interested?"

"Sure," she said.

Evangeline arrived a few minutes later dressed in an austere black dress that accentuated her unusual pallor.

"Been doing too much logic, Vange," Ecco said to her. "We have to find our way to the Yucatan for the winter breezes."

"And to see the ruins, too, you decadent beach bum," Evangeline responded with a smile.

FAKES

Ecco felt that practice and conditioning were as necessary to the omniheurist as to any athlete. One day he proposed that we enter a puzzle contest. The puzzle was the following.

You are given 20 coins. Some are fake and some are real. If a coin is real, it weighs between 11 and 11.1 grams. If it is fake, it weighs between 10.6 and 10.7 grams. You are allowed 15 weighings on a scale (not a balance). You are to determine which coins are real and which are fake.

"What do you make of it, Professor?" Ecco asked me. "The prize is significant."

"It seems quite hard," I said. "What makes it particularly hard is that if four coins weigh 44 grams, you could have three reals (weighing 11.1 grams) and one fake (weighing 10.7 grams) or you could have four reals (weighing 11 grams)."

"That does make it tough, I admit," said Ecco. He fell into one of those brooding silences that suggested deep concentration.

"You are a smart fellow, my friend," Ecco said teasing. "The problem you point out leads to the answer."

 How do you do it? (Solution on page 171.)

CHAPTER SIX

Fame

KNOWLEDGE COORDINATION I

> I know it and you know it, but do you know I know it?
> *—chapter subtitle from Evangeline's doctoral thesis.*

It was a rainy day in January and Ecco was muttering incomprehensibly as he slowly turned an unopened letter in his hands. He barely acknowledged Evangeline's entrance. I opened the door and she walked gracefully to a seat.

"What's the matter, Jacob? You seem in a sour mood today," she said.

"Look at the postmark on this letter," Ecco grunted in response. It was dated two months earlier; the return address was Olga Aronov, Leningrad University, Soviet Union. "Some of the letters from Olga never arrive. Others arrive like this one with edges curled.

"Olga and I have devised a test to see how often our letters are steamed open. This one was opened twice, presumably once here and once there. Government snoops."

Ecco broke the seal carefully and began to read. His anger seemed to soften as he read Olga's idiosyncratic script. Although their correspondence turned mostly on puzzles and mathematics, there was always a suggestion of something more personal.

This one read: "Winter is fully upon us. The nights bring blizzards and the Baltic has frozen over. Sometimes the winds are calm and the cold reminds me of our walk in the parks of Stockholm, during which you taught me combinatorial catastrophe theory.

"I have run across a nice problem in the literature that I want to share with you. It is called the Coordinated Attack Problem.

"There are two allied generals A and B whose camps are on the opposite sides of a ridge. They can communicate with each other only by carrier pigeon. The pigeons sometimes get lost or killed by birds of prey.

"The generals must decide whether or not to attack the enemy the next morning. Whatever they decide, either they both attack or neither attacks, because an attack by just one would lead to disaster.

"Now, suppose general A decides that the moment is propitious, so he sends a message via carrier pigeon to general B, saying 'Attack at dawn.' Without receiving confirmation, general A won't attack, so he asks general B to acknowledge the message. General B sends his acknowledgment."

Evangeline, Ecco, and I looked at each, predicting the next question.

 (1) Will any sequence of successful acknowledgments and counteracknowledgments lead them to attack? If so, how many will be required? (Solution on page 171.)

"As soon as A receives the acknowledgment from B, he knows that A knows of his intent. So, both know the intent of A," I said.

"Yes," said Ecco, "but B knows that A won't attack without the acknowledgment. Since B is not sure that his acknowledgment will reach A, B himself won't attack until he knows that A has in fact seen the acknowledgment. So, A must send an acknowledgment to the acknowledgment."

"How does Olga end the letter?" Evangeline asked.

Ecco read on: "Maybe there is a way to parlay this surprising result into permanent world peace. —Olga"

"Just as I thought," said Evangeline, as she answered the question and gave a beautiful proof.

"There's a nice variation," Evangeline continued. "Suppose the armies have scouts on top of the ridge who light a beacon for a few seconds each time a carrier pigeon successfully makes a trip from one general to the other. Suppose both generals can see the beacon."

(2) How many successful carrier pigeon trips are required then?

Ecco found the answer quickly, but was still pensive. "It's remarkable. One can prove these results and understand every step of the proof, but still not believe the result. Our brains — with the possible exception of Evangeline's — have not evolved to deal in a facile way with knowledge about other people's knowledge about our knowledge."

KNOWLEDGE COORDINATION II

"It's good that Olga's letter has gotten you to think about such problems, Jacob, because I need your help on one," Evangeline said. "You see, your friend the Director realized that my thesis has to do with knowledge logics, so he has asked me to work with you on an 'innocent-sounding problem.'"

"My friend, indeed," said Ecco. "I suppose he told you that I'd be grumpy today as well, did he?"

"Well, he did mention the possibility," Evangeline responded. "Come to think of it, I was surprised that he brought it up. Do you think he knows about the letter-opening?"

"And that I know when they open letters?" asked Ecco rhetorically. "Let's just hope that he made a lucky guess. Did he tell you the problem or will he come to present it himself?"

"Yes, he told me, and it is very hard," said Evangeline as she bent over her notes. "Here's how it goes.

"There are 13 logicians in a room, all wearing jackets. On the front of each logician is a name tag and all the logicians have different names. On the back of some of the jackets is a big X. Each of the logicians can see the back of everyone else's jacket, but not his own. Initially, someone comes into the room and says, 'At least one of you has an X on his back.' The problem is for each logician to figure out whether he has an X or not.

"They do this in the course of several rounds. In each round, the logicians who have not yet decided whether they have an X on their backs speak in alphabetical order. Each logician either says:

I don't know whether I have an X on my back, or

I don't have an X on my back, or

I do have an X on my back and at least one other logician does also but has not yet said that he does or

I do have an X on my back and all other logicians who do have already said so.

They are not allowed to say anything else.

"As soon as a logician decides, that is, announces, that he does or doesn't have an X on his back, he stops speaking. This is what happens. In the first round, four people decide. In the second round, three people decide. One decider in the second round says there are more X's. In the third round, the remaining six decide."

 Which logicians have X's on their backs? (Solution on page 172.)

"I suppose we may assume that the logicians are good logicians and never lie," Ecco said. "Otherwise, we have no hope."

Evangeline nodded agreement. "Also," she said, "they come to the correct conclusion." Ecco and Evangeline solved it in the course of an hour.

"Why do you think the Director should be interested in such a problem?" I asked.

"It's very strange," said Evangeline. "When is it the case that someone can observe a certain property about all other people but not see it about himself?"

Ecco nodded in agreement. "Maybe it's some new way of expressing the key to a code. Given a long sequence of digits, the solution to this puzzle might say which digits are important to the code."

My head was already spinning in confusion. The solution was not at all easy.

"The Director said he hoped we would come to some conclusion this afternoon," Evangeline said, looking at her watch. "You'll have to give it to him, because I've got a rehearsal to go to."

$$-3-$$

THE COURIERS PROBLEM

Big Brother is watching you, but Big Brother has brothers, too.
  —*graffiti in Washington Square Park, New York City.*

Shortly after Evangeline left, there was a knock on the door. It was the Director. Had he waited for Evangeline to leave? He didn't say. He listened carefully to Ecco's explanation of the solution to the second knowledge coordination puzzle. When he understood, he paused for a moment.

"I hope you're not tired, Dr. Ecco and Professor Scarlet, because I have a new puzzle for you. We trust that you will not divulge this to anyone."

"It would be hard for me to tell Olga, wouldn't you say, Mr. Director?" Ecco asked. The Director ignored the question. Resisting the natural and polite human tendency to answer questions must be part of the training of secret-misers.

"There are five parts to the design of a new top secret code: A, B, C, D, and E," the Director explained. "If the enemy gets all five, we will be in big trouble. But he can acquire any four of the five without danger to us. We want to communicate all five parts to our agent in country X. Four parts would be as useless to our agent as to our enemy. We are willing to use eight couriers. We are sure that no more than two will get caught. When a courier gets caught, we assume the enemy gets possession of all the parts he carries.

"We don't really know what to do. For example, if we send eight couriers, five with one part of the code design each, and one gets caught, our agent will not be able to understand the code. Someone in our bureau had the bright idea that we should make copies of the five parts and give them to the eight couriers. We can make copies, but we don't know how to distribute them. Obviously, sending all copies with all couriers gives the enemy a chance to break our code."

Dr. Ecco said, "Well, Mr. Director, if you want a solution with eight couriers, here is one."

 (1) Can you find a solution (there are several) with eight couriers such that no two carry all five parts and any six couriers do? (Solution on page 173.)

The Director understood Dr. Ecco's proof. Smiling, he asked, "What do you mean by 'if you want a solution with eight couriers'? Are you suggesting you can do better?"

"Yes," said Ecco.

"Well, there you're wrong. A top secret memo recently appeared in which one of our scientists proved that there is no way to solve this problem with fewer than eight couriers. The proof goes like this. Each part must be carried by three couriers in order for our agent to get all parts. That way, our agent will get the code even if two couriers are captured. Also, to prevent the enemy from getting the secret from two couriers, no courier should carry three or more parts. That means 15 parts have to be carried by people who can carry no more than two each. So we need eight couriers."

 Before reading on, do you understand and agree with this argument?

"But, Mr. Director," I said as he finished, "this so-called proof makes an unwarranted assumption. The requirement that no two couriers carry between them all five parts does not imply that no courier may carry three or more parts. It is at least theoretically possible that one courier could carry three parts and others could carry two, but combining the parts carried by any two would yield only four different parts."

The Director looked at me with a slight smile. "In theory, Professor Scarlet, you may be right. But I am a practical man." He turned to leave, bringing his hand to his head in a mock salute.

"Wait, Mr. Director," said Ecco. "Here is a practical application of the professor's theoretical observation." Ecco wrote rapidly and handed the Director a piece of paper. "Seven couriers are quite sufficient. No two of them carry all five parts. Any five of them carry all five parts."

 (2) Construct a solution requiring only seven couriers. Use the professor's objection as a clue.

The Director studied the piece of paper for a moment. His jaw dropped. "I'll wring that scientist's neck," he growled.

"Don't be too hard on him," said Ecco. "After all, he does work for a secret agency." The Director slammed the door behind him.

A few days later, the Director reappeared. "Well, Ecco," he said, "so even you have your limits. The supervisor of the scientist with the bogus proof is prepared to fire him. Not only was the proof wrong for seven, but the supervisor says that he can solve the problem with six couriers. Yet you said seven was the minimum."

"Has he shown you his strategy?" asked Ecco.

"No, it has too high a classification," the Director replied.

"I hope its classification doesn't permit anyone besides the supervisor to see the method," said Ecco.

"What do you mean by that?" asked the Director, adjusting his tie.

Ecco turned to me and smiled. "The axiom once again, right, Professor?" I nodded, knowing what would come next. Ecco wrote some quick notes on paper. "The axiom, Mr. Director," he said, "is that secrecy is the sand castle of the incompetent.

"This supervisor cannot possibly be correct. There is no way to send six or fewer couriers in such a way that your agent can reconstruct the five-part code from the parts of any four agents, yet the enemy cannot reconstruct the code from any two."

 (3) Can you prove that Dr. Ecco is right?

After the Director left, Ecco turned to me. Noticing my furrowed brow, he said, "You've thought of the unsolved problem here, too, haven't you, Professor?"

"Yes. It is rather troubling," I said. "The question is, if you could divide up the code into any number of pieces, what is the smallest number of couriers you could possibly need, given that two might be captured?"

"Exactly," said Ecco. "Four couriers are not enough, because if any two couriers know the full message, then the enemy is sure to get it if he captures two. But five is still conceivable. But can it be done? I would be very much surprised if we don't receive a call in a few days offering us that question exactly."

Ecco was right, but his timing was off. That afternoon the Director called again, the phone beeping as always.

"Ecco, we only have five couriers available," he said. "Can you dig deeper into your bag of tricks to figure out a way to do it with just five, even though two still might be captured? Suppose that the code can be broken up into any number of parts, k, such that no one can reconstruct the code from any $k - 1$ parts."

Ecco took a few hours, but he solved it.

 (4) Can you solve this problem with five couriers?

ROAD WORK

The gentleman who entered in the elegant dark suit was preceded by bodyguards. They searched the room carefully with handheld electronic jammers. While waiting, the gentleman looked at Ecco and me as if to comfort us. He was clearly used to this introductory delay, but sensed that private citizens were not.

Little did I imagine then that this elegant figure would bring so many interesting problems, or bring Ecco so much fame. Ecco deserved it, as you will see.

"Señores," he said, "please excuse all the security, but one must take precautions."

"Yes, of course, Señor Presidente," said Ecco, extending his hand. After shaking hands, Ecco turned toward me. "Presidente Carballero, this is my good friend and colleague, Professor Scarlet." I shook his gloved hand, feeling horribly underdressed. Ecco looked unapologetic about his jeans and polo shirt as he motioned el Presidente to a seat.

"I called you, Dr. Ecco," he said, "to discuss the future of our beautiful capital city. It is laid out in the European style with a great plaza on which there is a rotary and several roads directed radially away from the rotary."

The president paused briefly as he showed us aerial views of the city. The view at sunrise was majestic, but the view at sundown showed cars and trucks in a bumper-to-bumper snarl. Only the central plaza had no traffic jam.

"These photographs tell the whole story, Señores," he continued. "Traffic jams are ruining the city. We will soon build a subway, but in the meantime we must do something about the roads.

"My traffic engineers tell me that converting the radial roads from two-way to one-way would more than double their capacity. Others say that their plan would lengthen some one-block trips to eight-block journeys. They say that they will agree to the conversion, only if no trip is lengthened by more than one block. I've come to you to see whether that is possible. Since the time to go around the rotary at the central plaza is short, we won't count that time."

"Please show me the road plan," said Ecco. "Here it is, Señor," said the president.

Ecco looked at the drawing for a few minutes. There were streets between the plaza and each of the points, A, B, C, D, E, and F. There were also roads of about the same length between A and B, between B and C, between C and D, between D and E, and between E and F. Ecco took a piece of scrap paper and began drawing lines, his head bent over the paper.

Finally, he looked up at Presidente Carballero and said, "Sorry, sir, it can't be done. Please let me explain. The reason is in fact quite subtle."

 (1) *Show that Ecco is right. (Solution on page 175.)*

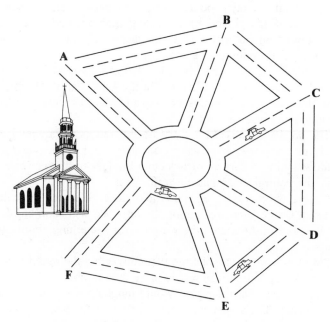

Figure 13 Capital plaza and surrounding roads.

Presidente Carballero looked very disappointed. Ecco suddenly smiled and said, "But the situation is not so bad. I can show that no trip will be more than doubled."

 (2) Give a design that doesn't more than double the length of any trip. Be careful!

"Thank you, Señor. That should satisfy everyone, especially since most trips in your design are in fact lengthened by only one road," said Presidente Carballero. "Allow me to return tomorrow to discuss our country road plans. Tonight I must join my friends at the Victorian Club."

COUNTRY ROADS

Presidente Carballero came back the next day in a dress military uniform. He looked imposing with his two rows of medals.

"This next problem, Señor Ecco, may be less glamorous, since few outsiders go into our provinces, but it is of great importance to my country," said el Presidente. "My country has a huge area with flat and desolate terrain. We have been able to build essentially only one-lane roads between the main cities. People drive on these roads in both directions, but whenever two vehicles meet, one must stop on the side to let the pass. Sometimes, however, people don't stop, and there are terrible accidents. Even when they do stop, the journey takes a long time.

"My engineers again tell me that making the roads one way will shorten travel times, even for travelers who would have to use one more road than they now use. I don't want the people to have a longer trip because of our well-intentioned improvements.

"On the other hand, we are a poor country, so we would prefer not to have to build any new roads. If we must build, then we would prefer to build a short road rather than a long one.

"Every road is very close to 100 miles long and is quite straight. There are roads between A and B, B and C, A and C, B and D, C and D, C and E, and D and E. A and D are about 170 miles apart, as are B and E. Unfortunately, I don't have a map."

Ecco thought about the president's description and began drawing a map of his own. "No map is necessary. Only one configuration is really possible. The distance between A and E is nearly 200 miles," said Ecco.

 (1) How does Ecco know? Remember that he is an excellent geometrician. The other parts of this puzzle do not depend on your knowing how to solve this part. (Solution on page 176.)

"You are right, Señor Ecco," said the president. "Now, can you make all the roads one way without adding more than one road length to any journey? It would be excellent if you added no

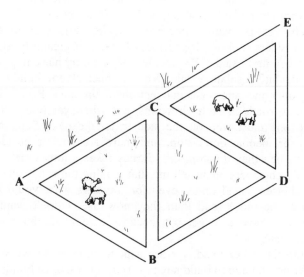

Figure 14   Rural roads in Presidente Carballero's country.

new roads either. My engineers think that any solution requires 200 miles worth of road. In fact, between A and E."

Ecco thought for a moment. "Well, your engineers are certainly right; some road building is necessary. Let me demonstrate this to you in a short argument."

 (2) Try to make a convincing argument.

After Ecco gave his argument, the president sighed. "Is it 200 miles then, Señor Ecco? Every mile costs us much of our wealth."

Ecco thought a moment, then answered. El Presidente seemed heartened, but I couldn't hear what the answer was.

 (3) Figure out which road to add, how long it should be, and show that your solution works.

"Thank you, Señor Ecco," said El Presidente Carballero. "We will see each other again tomorrow I hope. Tonight I attend the benefit at the Met, your beautiful opera house."

—⑥—
SUBWAY LAYOUT

His excellency, el Presidente Carballero, appeared at the door early the next morning. His clothes were casual but expensive. He was to meet his friends for lunch in Southampton out on Long Island. His private helicopter was waiting at the East River heliport.

After the ritual with the bodyguards, he began. "Please feel free to take your time with this problem, Dr. Ecco, because the problem looks as if it will take quite a few days, if it can be solved at all. We want to build a subway that will connect the whole of our capital city. As always, the economy is critical. So, we are willing to have a ride take some time as long as it is possible to get from any place to any other.

"The sheet shows you the cost in billions of gold pesos to build the leg between every two points. There are eight points

Cost in gold pesos and travel time for subway routes

Point	Point	Cost	Time
1	2	17	3
1	3	15	5
1	4	10	2
1	5	15	6
1	6	18	3
1	7	20	4
1	8	14	2
2	3	14	5
2	4	16	4
2	5	11	6
2	6	13	8
2	7	11	3
2	8	16	2
3	4	14	1
3	5	13	4
3	6	19	3
3	7	10	8
3	8	12	2
4	5	11	4
4	6	13	2
4	7	21	1
4	8	17	4
5	6	15	3
5	7	10	5
5	8	9	1
6	7	20	2
6	8	11	4
7	8	15	3

altogether. For example, laying a track between point 1 to point 2 costs 17 billion gold pesos. We represent that fact by the three numbers 1, 2, 17. Every leg carries passengers in both directions. The sheet also shows the time, in minutes, that it would take to travel between the two points, but we will return to that later. Here are the numbers."

Ecco took the sheet from the president's hands.

"Presidente, each one of these connections are two way, right?" Ecco asked.

"Yes, Señor," said Presidente Carballero.

"And there only has to be a route from one point to any other? The route may go through many intermediate stations, right?" asked Ecco.

"Correct," said el Presidente. "My own engineers came up with a 81-billion-peso solution, which they said was the best possible. They used a computer. But I wanted a second opinion. I do not, of course, expect you to solve the problem today, sir. I will return in two days."

Ecco probably didn't even hear the last few words. He was scribbling and crossing things out on a separate piece of paper. I offered the president tea and cookies. He took them graciously and began a highly informed discussion of the strengths and weaknesses of the various members of the Danish soccer team. They were to play his country's team the next day.

As the president was about to leave, Ecco spoke up. "But Presidente Carballero," he said, "I think that I can lay out your subway for quite a bit less."

 (1) Try to solve the problem. Give the point-to-point connections that you plan to use. (Solution on page 177.)

"But how did you solve the problem so quickly, Señor Ecco?" asked el Presidente. "You are world renowned for your cleverness, but there are so many possibilities."

Ecco said, "I will be glad to explain it to you, your excellency. The method was invented by the mathematician Kruskal in 1956. If you will allow me?"

"If you think I will understand," the president said with a chuckle, "please proceed."

 (2) Try to describe a very simple and quick method that yields a minimum-cost subway system connecting all stations.

"Now, Señor Ecco," said el Presidente, "perhaps you can solve an even more difficult problem. The center of our city is station 1. Ideally, our subway system should minimize the time it takes to get from any other point to the center. Can you give me a layout that allows everyone to travel to the center in five minutes of travel time? Ignore delays due to changing or waiting for trains. With that constraint, try to discover the cheapest layout possible. It would be excellent if it cost less than the 100 billion pesos, which the construction consultants told me would be the minimum."

Ecco thought for some time. In fact, Presidente Carballero had to leave for his engagement in Southampton before Ecco had finished. When he returned, Ecco greeted him warmly.

"I think you'll like my answer," said Ecco.

 (3) Ecco's answer cost 91 billion pesos. Try to figure out one at least that good.

Presidente Carballero was delighted. "My country would be honored to host you in our independence day celebrations in the spring. I will present you with our National Medal," he said.

Ecco thanked him graciously.

CHAPTER SEVEN

Vanished

—①—
PUZZLE-MAD KIDNAPPER

If a rock falls on your head, it's your fault for walking where rocks can fall.

— *from Ecco's notebook, "Societal Attitudes."*

This book has taken some time to write. Ecco has given his permission if only to dispel the myths that have come to surround him. The *Times* didn't help by publishing its front page story, "'Omniheurist' wins National Prize," about Ecco's accomplishments on behalf of Presidente Carballero. The lavish praise ascribed almost supernatural powers to Ecco.

The calls to Ecco now became a flood. He hired an answering service and changed his phone number. He even asked me to follow him home one day to see whether he was being followed. It was hard to tell since no one followed him the whole way. However, we repeated the attempt a few times and I thought I saw the same people. I kept this to myself to avoid alarming Ecco.

He became suspicious of everyone. Always reclusive, he refused case after case. In fact, he accepted only one client in the following month, in what must be the most intellectually difficult as well as emotionally wrenching of his career.

The woman introduced herself only as a wealthy heiress. "You will be amply rewarded if you help me, Dr. Ecco. You needn't know my name." She then proceeded to tell a story about her talented actor-son who had eschewed the family business and "who then fell in with the wrong crowd."

She said, "One day last month he disappeared altogether. I

didn't know anything about him until I received this most disturbing call from a man who introduced himself only as Baskerhound.

"He gave me a kind of riddle. 'I am thinking of a number between 1 and 2000. If you can determine what the number is in 15 or fewer questions, we will release your son. Otherwise we will kill him. I will answer each question with a yes or no. But, beware, I may lie once. Also, I will answer your questions only after you have asked all of them.'

"Dr. Ecco, what am I to do?" said the heiress sobbing loudly, exhausted from her efforts to present the story calmly.

Ecco thought for a few minutes, then said, "If I understand the scenario correctly, we ask him all the questions at once. Then he answers them all (starting after we have finished the last question). Then we must tell him his number. Is that correct?"

"Yes," said the heiress. "That is exactly correct. But how, Dr. Ecco? How?"

"That's the Baskerhound of Princeton," Ecco said, turning to me. "He dropped out of university life when he felt that his greatness was insufficiently recognized. He turned to masterful computer crimes and now to kidnapping. He is remarkably clever and the police have never been able to make their charges stick. Fortunately for us, he has a weakness for puzzles.

"Madam, let me think about your problem for an hour. I think I see some hope."

The lady left after looking at her watch. "We must answer him in three hours, Dr. Ecco. Please think well."

After she left, Ecco fell silent. When the hour was nearly up, Ecco just shook his head. I could see he had not made much progress.

Suddenly, I remembered a parlor game question by Professor Turab of Columbia University. "It only takes 11 questions to find the answer for 2000 numbers without lying, even if the respondent only answers all the questions at the end," I said. "We might rephrase the problem as follows: There are 11 coins numbered 1 to 11. Each is either heads or tails, face up or face down. If lying is forbidden, we can just ask about the setting of each coin and collect all the answers at the end."

(1) What are the corresponding 11 questions that would solve Baskerhound's problem, assuming he told the truth but waited until the last question before answering any of the questions? (Solution on page 178.)

"Very clever, Professor," said Ecco solemnly. "But the rephrased problem is still tough. If he doesn't lie, we figure out the number after 11 questions. If he were only allowed to lie once, we could certainly figure out the answer within 33 questions, but that's more than twice what he allows."

 (2) How does Dr. Ecco know that 33 questions are sufficient for the problem about coins?

Ecco sat back and stared at the ceiling. I went out for a walk. I found a simple way to get our problem down to 23 questions, but that still left eight to go. Anyway, that would have required him to answer each question as it was posed.

 (3) How would you solve the coin problem with only 23 questions, but with immediate answers to each question?

When I returned, Ecco was busily drawing on a sheet of paper. The distressed lady returned in two and one-half hours. Ecco was smiling, holding a single piece of paper in his hand. Finally, he stopped and showed me his list of questions.

"Professor, your observation has really paid off. Here are the questions for the 11-coin problem. Since your observation did all the rest of the work, you will please translate these questions into questions about numbers."

(4) How would you solve the coin problem in 15 questions, where the respondent only answers after you've asked all your questions and may lie once?

Baskerhound proved to be a man of his word. The lady's son was released and he even wrote a note promising never to engage in any criminal activity against her family again. The note also included the menacing postscript: "Careful, Ecco, your days are numbered."

MYSTERY

The sad news is well known: Ecco has disappeared. Some say he's dead. Others say they've seen him. The newspapers follow the thinnest leads about Ecco, no matter in what remote corner of the world. They all turn out to be fabrications, mistakes, or just unverifiable.

In the meantime, omniheurists are popping up all over and police academies are preparing courses based on what they call the Eccoan Methods. Ecco saw it coming. "There are two reasons I'm not interested in fame," he once told me. "The personal one is that I would lose all privacy and would be harried by the press and other time-wasters. The second reason is societal. When a spotlight is turned on a person's life, even the most trivial details are highlighted. Instead of discovering the ephemeral playfulness that leads me to my solutions, people will try to distill tricks from the solutions themselves. They will popularize the tricks to an audience eager for bite-sized pieces of how-to knowledge. But the tricks are the result, not the source. It's like trying to sell the clock that registered the winner of a swimming race. And those are the high-class popularizers. The real charlatans will hold my idiosyncratic habits to be responsible. Now, windsurfing is not the road to omniheurism."

But I'm digressing. Here is the story of Ecco's disappearance as far as I know.

After the Baskerhound affair, Ecco became more and more withdrawn. I knew he was overwhelmed with appeals for help, most of which were inappropriate to his skills. But still I did not understand his glum looks. Finally, one day he called Evangeline and me to his apartment. He told us that he thought that he was in danger, but he did not know from whom or exactly why.

A letter had come with a photograph. The letter said:

wnwjqgfw cfgok ow sjw svnwjksjawk. af ljmlz, ow sjw xjawfvk. ow oadd ywl qgm, vj. wuug.

Code again.

Ecco showed me the photograph. "Your seatmate on the plane back from India," I observed.

"That's right," said Ecco. "I don't know whom or what he works for, but as you recall he knows a lot about me. Anyway, I don't want either of you to be in danger. Don't come by or call for a week. By then I should know what to do. If I should disappear, please attend any gold auctions you can hear about."

That was the last either of us saw of him. I have checked, but he hasn't left the country, at least not under his own passport. All I have are questions. Did Baskerhound (who is still at large) make good on his threat? Did a security agency put him in protective custody? The Director claims to be ignorant, but I wonder. Ecco's interests and clients came from such a wide sphere. All of a sudden, they all seemed suspect.

There's another possibility. Could Ecco be hiding? Maybe he didn't want to tell Evangeline and me in order to protect us.

The evidence for this possibility is not overwhelming. He has drawn no checks on his bank account and has taken no belongings — except perhaps one.

About three months after Ecco's disappearance, I attended an auction of cast gold art, according to his instructions. The last item offered was remarkably similar to the drilling rig the Houston oil equipment dealer had given Ecco as payment. I remember hearing at the time that it was made to order. I inquired about the buyer, who was a Mr. John Halley.

I hurried to Ecco's apartment. It was messy as usual and the shoebox that Ecco had used to store the rig was nowhere to be found. Nor was the rig itself.

A few days later, I visited Halley. "What business is it of yours, sir?" Halley said indignantly when I asked why he got the piece.

Pressing him led nowhere. "I do not get mixed up in disappearing people, sir," he said. "Now you will please leave or I will call the police."

I left and I still don't know what to do. In spite of his iciness, Halley seemed to have no motive to harm Ecco. On the other hand, there was something disturbing about Halley. He reminded me of one of Ecco's clients — the treasure hunter Hanson, I think. But how could that be?

Evangeline and I have been trying to break the code in the three messages Ecco received. The first message was left in Ecco's apartment after we returned from Columbia Gorge:

nwjq udwnwj sjwf'l qgm?

The second one was stuffed in my briefcase on our return from India:

ow fwwv qgmj zwdh, sdgfw.

The third one came by letter:

wnwjqgfw cfgok ow sjw svnwjksjawk. af ljmlz, ow sjw xjawfvk.
ow oadd ywl qgm, vj. wuug.

I think there's a clue in these messages.

Solutions
to Puzzles

CHAPTER ONE

① MINORITY RULES

(1) The strategy is to make the most popular proposals face one another first. C will win if the elections are held in the order: D vs. B (D wins 51 to 49), A vs. D (A wins 66 to 34), A vs. C (C wins 51 to 49).

(2) No, if the opposition chooses the proposals in the second election, then B or D will win. Notice first that B wins against every proposal except D. So, if D loses in the first round, B will win. If D survives the first round and both A and C are still available, then the opposition pits A against C in the second round. C will win, but will then lose to D in the third round.

The remaining possibility is that D survives and only one of A or C survive the first round. This means that B must survive as well. So, in the second round the opposition pits B against the surviving choice of A or C. That will leave only B and D for the third round.

(3) We've shown how to make C win. A wins with the ordering B vs. C, D vs. B, and A vs. D. D wins using A vs. B, B vs. C, and B vs. D. B wins using A vs. D, A vs. B, and B vs. C.

② THE TOWER OF LEGO

(1) 13 weeks. In one week, there could be 500 stacks, each 2 pieces high. In two weeks, there could be 250 stacks, each 4 pieces high. In three weeks, 125 stacks, 8 high. In four weeks, 62

stacks, 16 high and 1 stack, 8 high. In five weeks, 31 stacks, 32 high and 1 stack, 8 high. In six weeks, 15 stacks, 64 high and 1 stack, 40 high. In seven weeks, 7 stacks, 128 high and 1 stack, 104 high. In nine weeks, 3 stacks, 256 high (remember the 1-week delay) and 1 stack, 232 high. In eleven weeks, 1 stack, 512 high and 1 stack, 488 high. In thirteen weeks, a 1-kilometer stack.

(2) 20 weeks.

Discussion: This puzzle shows that parallelism has its limits. The tower can't be built in a day, no matter how rich Hank Alfred is. In computer science, the argument that shows this is called a fan-in argument. In the first problem, there are 1000 input towers and one output tower incorporating all those inputs. Because combining two smaller towers into a larger one is the basic operation (it has fan-in of two), each parallel execution of this operation can reduce the number of needed towers only by a factor of 2. That is why 10 parallel executions are needed.

③ ODD DOORS PROBLEM

Each door has two sides. For ease of visualization, imagine that there is a doorknob on each side. So, each door has two doorknobs. No matter how many doors there are, there must be an even number of doorknobs all together, say n of them. Once you enter the labyrinth with three doors, there are $n - 3$ doorknobs facing all the rooms in the interior, because three doorknobs face the outside. This must be an odd number, since n is even. So, there must be an odd number facing some room in the three-door labyrinth.

The labyrinth with two doors does not necessarily have such a room. Since the senior Mr. Terrence said that young Lawrence should be able to figure out which one, only one labyrinth can have such a room. Therefore, the three-door labyrinth must be it.

Discussion: This illustrates a combinatorial principle known as the Parity Principle. The total number of doorknobs facing interior rooms is odd, so one room must have an odd number of doorknobs.

④ THE COACH'S DILEMMA

(1) Divide the eight players into four groups of two each. Have each player play the other in his group. That requires four hours. Now rank four of the players: Take two groups of two; call them X and Y. Have the best player of X play the best player of Y. The winner is the best of those two groups. The loser then plays the worst player of the other group. The winner of the second game is second best. At this point, if the loser of the first game loses the second, then you have enough information to rank all four players in X and Y. Otherwise, the worst players of both groups must play to determine who is third best. So, ranking four players consisting of two pairs of ranked players takes at most three hours. To get two groups of four players takes at most six hours starting with ranked pairs.

The two ordered groups of four can be represented like so:

A	E
B	F
C	G
D	H

order from best to worst   order from best to worst

To complete the ranking, you follow seven steps:

1. A plays E. Say A wins:

B	E	A
C	F	
D	G	
	H	

2. B plays E. Say E wins:

B	F	A
C	G	E
D	H	

3. B plays F. Say F wins:

B	G	A
C	H	E
D		F

4. B plays G. Say G wins:

B	H	A
C		E
D		F
		G

5. B plays H. Say B wins:

C	H	A
D		E
		F
		G
		B

6. C plays H. Say C wins (if H had won, we'd be through):

D	H	A
		E
		F
		G
		B
		C

7. D plays H. Say D wins:

A
E
F
G
B
C
D
H

Thus, to rank eight players given two ranked groups of four players each takes at most seven hours. (You might try to show that given any two groups of ranked players of sizes x and y, you can rank them into one group of size $x + y$ in at most $x + y - 1$ hours.) So, the total time is $4 + 6 + 7 = 17$ hours. In fact, a more complicated technique discovered by Hugo Steinhaus and independently by Arthur Whitney leads to a 16 hour solution. Hint: try to rank 5 players in 7 hours first. More of a hint: Play 1 vs. 2 (say 1 wins). Play 3 vs. 4 (say 3 wins). Play 1 vs. 3 (say 1 wins). So far, this is entirely general. Now, try 5 vs. 3. There are two cases: 5 wins or 3 wins.

(2) Using four courts, we can rank the players in six hours. (See Figure 15.) We identify the courts as A, B, C, and D. Initially, we divide the eight players into four pairs and have each pair play at a court. We will explain where the winner and loser at each court plays in the next hour. Sometimes a player doesn't play during an hour, in which case we say that he sits out the hour.

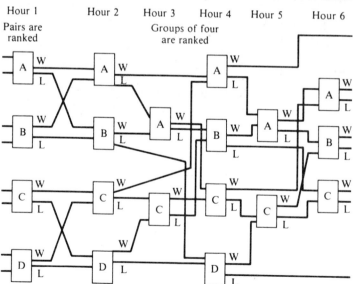

Figure 15 Here is where the winners and losers go in the six-hour ranking match.

After hour one:

> Winner at A stays at A. Loser at A goes to B.
> Winner at B goes to A. Loser at B stays at B.
> Winner at C stays at C. Loser at C goes to D.
> Winner at D goes to C. Loser at D stays at D.

After hour two:

> Winner at A sits out an hour, then plays at A in hour four.
> Loser at A stays at A.
> Winner at B goes to A. Loser at B sits out an hour, then plays
> at D in hour four.
> Winner at C sits out an hour, then plays at A in hour four.
> Loser at C stays at C.
> Winner at D goes to C. Loser at D sits out an hour, then goes
> to D.

After hour three:

> Winner at A goes to C. Loser at A goes to B.
> Winner at C stays at C. Loser at C goes to B.

After hour four:

> Winner at A is best player and is done. Loser at A stays at A.
> Winner at B goes to A. Loser at B sits out an hour, then plays
> at C in hour six.
> Winner at C sits out an hour, then plays at A in hour six.
> Loser at C stays at C.
> Winner at D goes to C. Loser at D is the worst player and is
> done.

After hour five:

> Winner at A stays at A. Loser at A goes to B.
> Winner at C goes to B. Loser at C stays at C.

After hour six:

We already know the best and worst player from hour four. The
second best player is the winner at A. The third best is the loser

at A. The fourth best player is the winner at B. The fifth best is the loser at B. The sixth best player is the winner at C. The seventh best is the loser at C.

(3) Whether there is a solution that works in five hours is still an open question.

Discussion: This illustrates two solutions to the sorting problem, a problem used in virtually every application of computers from computational geometry to data processing to artificial intelligence. The algorithm to solve problem (1) is merge-sort, whose invention is lost in folklore, although seminal computer designer John Von Neumann is said to have known it. The second algorithm is due to K. E. Batcher and is known as Batcher-sort.

A description of merge-sort may be found in any introductory algorithms textbook, such as *Data Structures and Algorithms* by Aho, Hopcroft, and Ullman (Reading MA: Addison-Wesley). Batcher-sort can be found in any of the new textbooks on parallel algorithms.

⑤ MAXIMUM FLOW

(1) Route assignments for 20 tons from Houston to Moscow:

Houston to Frankfurt — 3 tons
Houston to Paris — 11 tons
Houston to Rome — 3 tons
Houston to London — 3 tons
Rome to Moscow — 3 tons
London to Warsaw — 3 tons
Frankfurt to Warsaw — 4 tons
London to Paris — 0 tons
Paris to Frankfurt — 9 tons
Paris to Moscow — 2 tons
Frankfurt to Moscow — 8 tons
Warsaw to Moscow — 7 tons

(2) The answer is still 20 tons. Here was Ecco's explanation: "You can't put through a network more than can go through one of its cross-cuts. A cross-cut is a collection of routes (in this case, city-to-city flights) with the property that every ton passing through the network goes through exactly one of those routes."

A cross-cut are the routes from Houston to Rome, Warsaw to Moscow, Frankfurt to Moscow, and Paris to Moscow. No more than 20 tons can pass along these routes, and every ton must pass through exactly one of them.

(3) Add one more flight on the Warsaw to Moscow route, and three flights from Houston to Rome. The route from Rome to Moscow can take an additional 9 tons. The route from Houston to London to Warsaw can take another 3 tons.

Discussion: A good introduction to network flows, as this problem is called, is *Introductory Combinatorics* by Kenneth P. Bogart (Belmont, CA: Pitman Publishing).

⑥ CRITICAL PATHS

(1) The first half of F, the first half of D, and E take 6.5 years. (See Figure 16.)

(2) Paying 15 million dollars to halve the times for B, D, and E reduces the total time to four years.

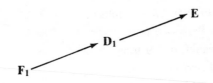

Figure 16 The critical path that the professor notices.

CHAPTER TWO

① SPIES AND ACQUAINTANCES

(1) If all the spies were telling the truth, there would be an odd number of acquaintanceships. Since every meeting produces two acquaintanceships, this cannot happen.

(2) A, B, C, D, and F must be honest. A must be telling the truth since no spy will claim to have met more people than he actually has met, and A claims to have met every other spy. If B is lying and in fact knows six, then G would have to be lying, which is two liars, but we have been told to expect only one liar. So A and B must be telling the truth. Therefore, F knows A and either B or C, since we know that F is not a liar. (See Figure 17.)

Assume F knows A and B alone. Now, C knows at least four others. These must include A and B. They cannot include F, so they must include two out of three of D, E, and G. If C has met E, then E is a liar, and if C has met G, then G is a liar. So C has met one of E and G. If C were lying and in fact knew five others, then C would know both E and G, giving us three liars. So we know that C is telling the truth. Since either E or G is a liar, D must be telling the truth. D knows only A, B, and C.

If F knows A and C alone, a similar argument leads to the same conclusion: either E or G is a liar.

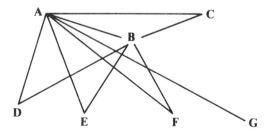

Figure 17 C must know two of D, E, and G.

② SPIES AND DOUBLE AGENTS

Both spies start with these statements:

> Exactly one of W, X, and Y is true.
> Exactly one of X, Y, and Z is true.

Since one of them is telling the truth, these two statements are true. So, either:

1. Both W and Z are true and both X and Y are false, or
2. Both W and Z are false and one of X and Y is true.

The reason is that if only one of W and Z, say W, were true, then X and Y would both be false, and then the statement involving the other one, say Z, would have no true members. If X or Y is true, then W and Z must be false. Otherwise, there would be more than one true member in each statement.

Yet spy A claims that exactly one of W and Z is false. This can't be true, so he's the double agent. Agent B tells us that exactly one of W, Y, Z is true, so Y must be true.

③ ROCKET ASSEMBLY

(1) No, it can't be done. There must be a conveyor belt from B to C, from C to D, from D to E, and from B to E. There must also be one from F to D and from F to I. So F cannot be inside the B, C, D, E region. But the A edge to G prevents F from being outside the A, C, D, E, G region. In that case, F cannot supply I. (See Figures 18 and 19.)

(2) Set up two construction stations for B. Put one station near C and one near E and H. Move F to the side with the second B station and surround the second B station with F, D, E, G, H, I. That solves all problems. (See Figure 20.)

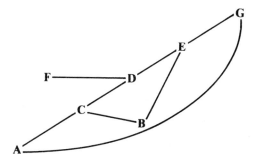

Figure 18 Layout of the assembly line before attaching H and I.

Discussion: The issue here is whether a graph is planar or not; that is, can it be drawn on a piece of paper without having any two edges cross. The best discussion of this problem comes from J. Hopcroft and R. E. Tarjan: "Efficient Planarity Testing," *Journal of the Association for Computing Machinery,* vol. 21, no. 4, pp. 549–568, October 1974.

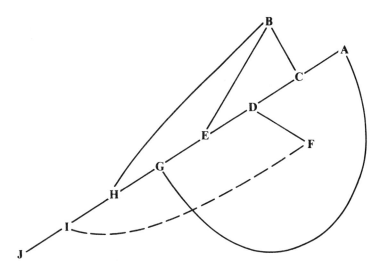

Figure 19 Assembly line with one crossover bridge, from F to I.

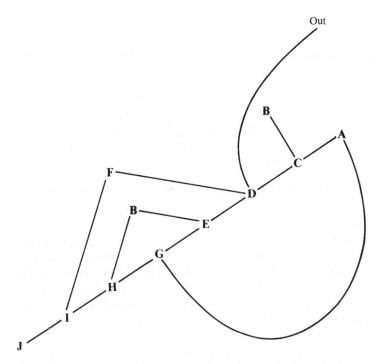

Figure 20 How duplicating station B will help eliminate bridges.

④ OFFSHORE OIL WELL

(1) The rate needed is 1.25 barrels per minute. In every 100 minutes the following would happen: send 100 barrels of oil from the rig to the shore (80 minutes); switch from oil to water (6 minutes); send 10 barrels of water (8 minutes); and switch back from water to oil (6 minutes).

(2) Increasing the size of the water drum to 14.4 barrels would permit a rate of 1.2 barrels per minute. Send 144 barrels of oil in 120 minutes to shore. Wait 6 minutes for a changeover from oil to water. Send 14.4 barrels of water in 12 minutes. Then wait 6 minutes for a changeover from water to oil and begin again.

Discussion: This problem really is inspired by traffic intersections. How long should a traffic light cycle be?

CHAPTER THREE

① THE CAMPERS' PROBLEM

(1) Following Ecco's suggestion, send the counselor down one
path, three campers down another, three down a third, and two
down a fourth. Each group walks 20 minutes, determines
whether the campsite is there, then returns, and each camper
reports what he or she believes the result to be. The counselor
then makes a decision in the following manner. If the counselor
finds the campsite, he leads his campers toward it. If there is
disagreement within the two three-camper groups, believe the
majority opinion (there can be only one liar per group). If there is
disagreement within one group of three and one group of two,
take the majority opinion of the three and ignore the two. If there
is disagreement within only one group altogether, ignore the
responses of that group. If there is no disagreement within any of
the groups, ignore the group with two campers.

(2) With only seven campers, some pair of paths (call them A and
B) must be visited by only four campers and no counselor.
Suppose that neither the counselor nor the remaining campers
find the campsite along the paths they explore. If the distribution
is four for A and zero for B, then the group of four can come
back split, two saying yes and two saying no. The counselor
would not know whether A was right or B was right. If the
distribution is three for A and one for B, then any disagreement in A also leaves open both possibilities. If the distribution is two and two, then if both come back with the same
answer, the counselor again has no way to decide.

(3) With five potential liars, 17 campers are needed. The counselor again goes down one path alone. He sends six campers
down two paths and five down the remaining path. Here is how
to evaluate the responses.

If there is disagreement in none of the groups, ignore the group with five. If there is disagreement in one group, ignore that group. If there is disagreement in two or more groups, the counselor must think as follows: In each group with disagreement, count the number of campers in the minority (if the vote is three to three, then make the "minority" count be three). That number is the minimum number of liars in that group. In any group where the number of responses on the majority side is more than five minus the total of the minimum number of liars in all of the other groups, trust the majority. That procedure plus the findings of the counselor on the path he visits will always yield an answer about three of the four paths.

With only 16 campers, some pair of paths has only 10 campers. If five can lie, there is no solution that works.

(4) A plausible but unsuccessful approach to this problem would be to reason that the counselor can take care of two paths (call them A and B) in two rounds and the campers can handle at least one of the other two (C and D). Suppose the counselor doesn't find the campsite. The professor's first observation (that with four campers, no majority of truth tellers is ever guaranteed) suggests that the counselor cannot know for sure which of C or D has the campsite. Suppose the liars give answers consistent with C and the truth tellers with D. Since it is two against two, symmetry prevents a resolution.

The Professor's second observation suggests that affirmative responses from the campers should be treated differently from negative answers. Here's how:

In round 1, the counselor goes down A. All four campers go down B.

When all reunite, if the counselor found the campsite, then everyone goes to A. If three or four campers agree on B, then it is B. If three or four campers agree that it isn't B, then counselor checks C in the second round, and all campers rest.

Now the tough case. If two say it is down B and two say it isn't, then counselor explores B again. One of those who said it wasn't B should be sent down C. Now if the counselor finds it, then it is B. If the counselor fails to find it, then the camper who went down C must be telling the truth, because the liars were those who said it was down B.

Discussion: Computer circuits and wires fail on occasion and often fail only temporarily. Special methods to detect and correct such "intermittent" failures are built into the memory circuitry of most modern computers.

② PEBBLES AND PERSUASION

This easel layout scheme requires only five easels:

Easel 1: G, I, K, S, A, N
Easel 2: H, J, L, F, B, E, R
Easel 3: O, C, D, U
Easel 4: P, M
Easel 5: Q, T

Here is the presentation order:

G, H, O, I, J, P, K, L, Q, S, F, T, A, B, C, M, D, E, N, R, U.

Discussion: This problem is inspired by graph pebbling, a combinatorial game played on graphs. Placing a pebble corresponds to showing a chart. The rules of the pebbling game are as follows:

1. A pebble may be placed on a vertex (i.e., a chart can be shown) if and only if all its immediate predecessors (i.e., supporting assertions) have pebbles on them (i.e., are visible).
2. A pebble may always be removed from a vertex. Once that happens, the vertex may never have a pebble placed on it again.

That five easels are enough to solve this problem means that five pebbles can pebble the support graph. The simple game of pebbling has been used to prove deep results in computational complexity theory. A pioneering paper using pebbling called "On Time Versus Space" by J. E. Hopcroft, W. J. Paul, and L. G. Valiant appeared in the *Journal of the Association for Computing Machinery*, vol. 24, pp. 332–337, 1977. Complexity theory in general is presented in a broad context in Steven A. Cook's Turing Award Lecture, "An Overview of Computational Complexity" in the *Communications of the Association for Computing Machinery*, vol. 26, pp. 401–409, 1983.

③ THE ARCHITECT'S PROBLEM

Figure 21 shows a design that meets the requirements. The H pattern is at the center of the solution.

Discussion: Chip designers lay out binary trees using the H pattern since it is the most space-efficient method available. A mathematical description of its virtues may be found in *Compu-*

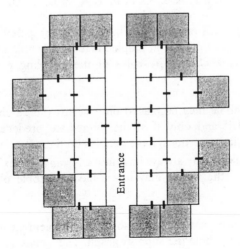

Figure 21 The layout of the Antarctic Research Station.

tational Aspects of VLSI by Jeffrey Ullman (Rockville, MD: Computer Science Press).

④ CIRCUITS CHECKING CIRCUITS

Figure 22 shows a 13-gate solution in detail. Number the inputs from 1 to 16. If more than one input has a 1, then at least one of the AND gates has a 1 at its output. This causes the rightmost OR gate to have a 1 at its output. Otherwise, either one or zero motors is receiving a "go" signal.

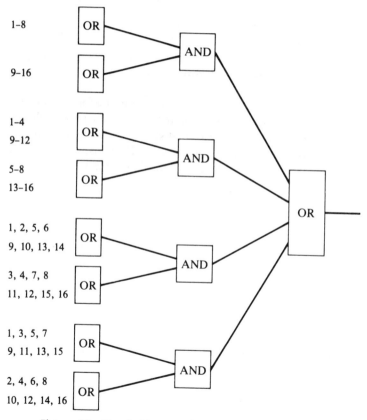

Figure 22 Ecco's 13-gate solution to Pollard's problem.

Discussion: This circuit is still at work inside certain large IBM computers.

⑤ GOSSIPING DEFENDERS

(1) Number the posts from 1 to 16. The following solution is not unique:

> First minute: pair 1 with 2, 3 with 4, 5 with 6, 7 with 8, 9 with 10, 11 with 12, 13 with 14, and 15 with 16.
> Second minute: pair 1 with 3, 2 with 4, 5 with 7, 6 with 8, 9 with 11, 10 with 12, 13 with 15, and 14 with 16.
> Third minute: pair 1 with 5, 2 with 6, 3 with 7, 4 with 8, 9 with 13, 10 with 14, 11 with 15, and 12 with 16.
> Fourth minute: 1 with 9, 2 with 10, 3 with 11, 4 with 12, 5 with 13, 6 with 14, 7 with 15, and 8 with 16.

(2) In one minute each post can know about the forces attacking two posts at most. In two minutes a post can only exchange information with another post that knows about the information in two posts, so it can only learn about four posts. Similarly, in three minutes, a post can learn about only eight posts.

(3) It is possible for the posts to communicate in four minutes, though it isn't easy. Here is one solution:

> First minute: pair 1 with 2, 3 with 4, 5 with 6, 7 with 8, and 9 with 10.
> Second minute: pair 1 with 7, pair 2 with 3, 4 with 9, 5 with 8, 6 with 10.
> Third minute: pair 1 with 9, pair 2 with 5, 3 with 10, 4 with 8, 6 with 7.
> Fourth minute: pair 1 with 2, 3 with 4, 5 with 6, 7 with 8, and 9 with 10.

(4) The simplest example is three posts rather than four. With four posts, one can solve the problem in two minutes. But with three, one needs three minutes.

⑥ DELICATE BALANCES

(1) Number the clamp types 1 through 18. In the first weighing, compare one clamp of types 1 and 2, 3 and 4, 5 and 6, 7 and 8, 9 and 10, 11 and 12, 13 and 14, 15 and 16. This leaves exactly 10 that could still be the lightest. Number those 1 to 10. In the second balancing, compare clamps of types 1 and 2, 1 and 3, 2 and 3, 4 and 5, 5 and 6, 4 and 6, 7 and 8, 9 and 10. (Here we are using the fact that each manufacturer has supplied several copies of its clamp.) This can only leave one of 1, 2, and 3; one of 4, 5, and 6; one of 7 and 8; and one of 9 and 10. We number these 1 to 4. In the last balancing, compare every one with every other: 1 and 2, 1 and 3, 1 and 4, 2 and 3, 2 and 4, 3 and 4.

(2) In fact, 18 is the best you can do. With 19, the first weighing leaves at least 11 possibilities. The second may leave 5. The last therefore may leave 2.

Discussion: Whereas this solution bears a superficial similarity with Coach McGraw's problem, it makes strong use of the fact that there are many copies of clamps used. The inspiration comes from work by Leslie Valiant that showed that finding the minimum of an unsorted array in parallel requires *log log* time. The theorems on stable sets in graphs that he used came from C. Berge's book, *Graphs and Hypergraphs* (New York: Elsevier North-Holland).

CHAPTER FOUR

① WAREHOUSES AND BARRELS

(1) The basic method would take three major phases. Since each phase requires 4 days, the whole operation would take 12 days.
    Phase one has four moves:

   1. Move barrels of chemicals c1, c2, c3, and c4 from warehouse w5 to warehouse w1, and move barrels of chemicals c5, c6, c7, and c8 from warehouse w1 to warehouse w5.

2. Do the same for warehouses w2 and w6.

3. Do the same for warehouses w3 and w7.

4. Do the same for warehouses w4 and w8.

Phase two has four moves:

1. Exchange barrels of chemicals c1, c1, c2, and c2 from warehouse w3 with barrels of chemicals c3, c3, c4, and c4 from warehouse w1.

2. Exchange the same chemicals between warehouses w2 and w4.

3. Exchange barrels of chemicals c5, c5, c6, and c6 from warehouse w7 with barrels of chemicals c7, c7, c8, and c8 from warehouse w5.

4. Exchange the same chemicals between warehouses w6 and w8.

Phase three has four moves:

1. Exchange the four barrels of chemical c2 in warehouse w1 with the four barrels of c1 in warehouse w2.

2. Exchange the four barrels of chemical c4 in warehouse w3 with the four barrels of c3 in warehouse w4.

3. Exchange the four barrels of chemical c6 in warehouse w5 with the four barrels of c5 in warehouse w6.

4. Exchange the four barrels of chemical c8 in warehouse w7 with the four barrels of c7 in warehouse w8.

(2) Each of these phases can be done in one day using four trucks.

(3) After the first day, a given warehouse can contain at most two barrels of any chemical. Therefore, after two days one warehouse (say, warehouse w1) can exchange only with another warehouse that has two barrels of the chemical that w1 needs. Therefore, w1 can contain only four barrels of its chemical by the end of the second day. So, one more day is needed to complete the total transfer.

② PARTY

(1) The fewest is six (Figure 23). Three or fewer is impossible, since no one could then have shaken the hands of three others. Four is not possible, since if three have shaken the hands of three others, then the fourth person must have shaken the hands of three others as well. Five is not possible for a similar reason. Six is possible. Let's say the six people are A, B, C, D, E, and F. Then the following handshakes may have occurred: A and B, B and C, C and D, D and E, E and F, A and C, A and E, and B and D.

(2) No, there could not be 21 people at such a party, nor any other odd number. Each time two people shake hands, each person adds one to the number of people he or she has shaken hands with. So, the total number of handshakes has increased by two (one for each person). If there were 21 people, then the total

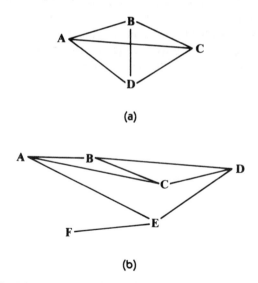

(a)

(b)

Figure 23 The smallest number of people who can be at the party. (a) There cannot be only four people at the party. If A, B, and C shake hands with three other people, then so does D. (b) Six people can be at the party.

number of handshakes would be $20 \times 3 + 1 = 61$. But that is impossible.

(3) Yes, there is a general pattern. Any even number greater than six will work. No odd numbers work. It is easy to see that six plus any multiple of four will work, since we could use the solution for (1) to show that six satisfy the properties and posit that each additional group of four people have only shaken hands among themselves. To see that eight plus any multiple of four works, just notice that if there were eight, A, B, C, D, E, F, G, and H, then the following pairs of people could have shaken hands: A and B, B and C, C and D, D and E, E and F, F and G, G and H, A and C, A and E, B and G, D and F.

③ CODE BREAKING

(1) This is a single substitution code. That is, each character in the encoded text translates to exactly one character in the plain text. To break the code, look for the most commonly occurring letters. These probably correspond to the letters that occur most often in English. The most frequently used letter in English is "e." The letters "i" and "t" are also frequently used. Decoding the remaining letters is a matter of hypothesizing and testing. Here is the translation:

> go to southern observation window of world trade center at ten am monday morning. aim center telescope towards ellis island. look for sailboat with blue sail. final message is on banner of sailboat in this code.

(2) buy ibm.

④ CODE INVENTION

Here is the code presented so that you can see that there is never any doubt about which letter is received.

D — dot dot (31)
G — dot dash dot (19)

A — dot dash dash (10)
B — dash dot (20)
E — dash dash dot dot (7)
F — dash dash dot dash (4)
C — dash dash dash (9)

Sending the average 100-word message takes 186 seconds using this code.

Discussion: The inspiration for this problem comes from Huffman's algorithm, which is a technique for finding a minimum weighted cost encoding of a set of code words into 1's and 0's. D. S. Parker describes the algorithm and its modern extensions in "Conditions for Optimality of the Huffman Algorithm," *SIAM Journal of Computing,* vol. 9, no. 3, 470–489.

⑤ SPACECRAFT MALFUNCTION

(1) At least two must be bad. Since E and C accuse one another of being faulty, at least one of them must be bad. Since F accuses B of being faulty, at least one of them must be bad. Since B accuses A of being faulty, at least one of them must be bad.

(2) If we know that no more than two are faulty, they would have to be B and C. To prove it, let's eliminate other possibilities.
    Suppose both D and E are faulty. Since either A or C is also faulty, that gives three faulty units, which is not possible.
    Suppose D or E is faulty, but not both. Since only one is faulty, F is good, so B is faulty as well. But either A or C is faulty, so there would then be three faulty units, which we assume is impossible.
    Therefore, neither D nor E is faulty. So, C is faulty, F is good, and B is faulty. B claims that A is faulty, but B cannot be trusted.
    So, the faulty ones are B and C.

⑥ ESCAPED TIGER

(1) Here is the solution showing the placements of keepers k1, k2, and k3 for seven 20-minute intervals. Note that at no time is there a free path from where the tiger might be to the entrance.

1. k1 at entrance; k2 at C; k3 at one of rooms leading from C.
2. k1 at entrance; k2 at other room leading from C; k3 at B.
3. k1 at A; k2 and k3 at the two rooms leading from B.
4. k1 at D; k2 at E; k3 at F.
5. k1 at G; k2 at K; k3 at J.
6. k1 at G; k2 at L; k3 at M.
7. k1 at H; k2 at I; k3 at room leading from M.

(2) This is the best possible time since even if each person explored a different room every 20 minutes, seven rounds would be needed to cover all 19 rooms. In six rounds, only $6 \times 3 = 18$ rooms could be searched.

(3) Send one keeper through the entire temple, while the other two wait in the entrance room. He should explore each group of rooms leading from the entrance, one group at a time. Using this method, that keeper would only catch the tiger by luck, since the tiger can run from room to room. However, the keeper can count how many rooms are in each group and draw a map of those rooms.

    The keepers will save the group with the most rooms for last; they thus choose one of the two smaller groups. Neither of the smaller groups can have more than 8 rooms. (Remember that there are 18 rooms in the three groups. Two of the three groups have an odd number of rooms, because of the connection rules. No two groups can have 9 rooms.) If the tiger is in either one of the smaller groups, then two keepers can find it.

    Here is how. As far as the search is concerned, there are two basically different configurations of 8 rooms. (See Figure 24.) In the first configuration, one keeper searches the single dead-end room at the left of the figure. If he doesn't find the tiger, both keepers advance to the 6 remaining rooms. Finding the tiger in those 6 rooms is easier for two keepers than finding the tiger in 8 rooms having the second configuration. So, we turn to that now.

    In the second configuration, one keeper searches a dead-end room on the right, then the room nearer the other keeper, then the other dead-end room in that branch. If that keeper doesn't find the tiger, both keepers advance to the remaining 4 rooms to the left. They search these in a similar manner.

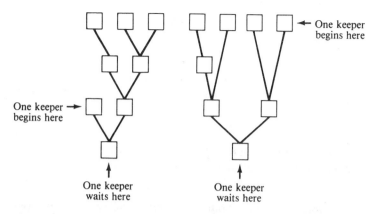

One keeper begins here

One keeper begins here

One keeper waits here

One keeper waits here

Figure 24 The two fundamentally different configurations of eight rooms that two keepers must search.

If the tiger is not in the two smaller groups of rooms, all three keepers advance on the first room of the third group. But now the problem is to find a tiger in at most 16 rooms. Again, two keepers should first explore the smaller group, which may have only 7 rooms, by the connection rules. The keepers continue to apply the same strategies for searching smaller groups of rooms until they find the tiger.

CHAPTER FIVE

① SPECULATIONS

(1) The most the holder of a call can receive from a trader is one dollar. Paying more for the privilege is a sure road to poverty.

(2) For every call you sell at 55 cents, buy 1 ounce of gold and one put at 30 cents. If the price increases by one dollar, you make one dollar on the gold and must pay a dollar to the purchaser of the call. You end up with a 25-cent profit on the options. If the price of gold stays the same, you also come out 25 cents ahead. If it goes down by one dollar, your profit on the put

and loss on the ounce of gold balances out again. You still make 25 cents.

(3) For every put you sell at 55 cents, sell 1 ounce of gold and buy one call at 30 cents. Again, you make 25 cents no matter what.

(4) For each pair of options, you receive 1.10 dollars. You only pay out one dollar at most.

(5) Anyone who buys both a put and a call will receive two dollars from him nine days out of ten. So, over a period of ten days, a person buying both a put and a call would pay Noriaty 12 dollars, and receive from Noriaty 18 dollars.

(6) The only truly safe price is one dollar. However, as long as Noriaty is in business, 61 cents would be safe. Stanley can buy a put from Noriaty at 60 cents each time he sells one. He can act similarly for a call.

② RAILROAD BLUES

(1) If you can't figure it out, read on in the text.

(2) It is possible. The train crew uncouples freight car 12 from the rest of the train. The locomotive drives down the siding with the first 12 freight cars. Then it backs out the other way (with the locomotive facing the new destination). The locomotive couples to the remaining seven cars (at this point the locomotive is sandwiched between the other cars in the train). The locomotive takes all the cars past the siding (toward the old destination) and then heads down the siding, pushing the seven as it goes. The locomotive uncouples from those seven and backs out. The locomotive and the original 12 cars pass the siding, going toward the new destination. The locomotive then backs those 12 down the siding until they can couple with the seven in the siding. The whole train can now go toward its next destination.

The train approaches the mine:

C - 6F - 12F - L

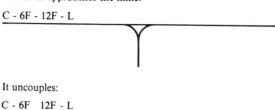

It uncouples:

C - 6F   12F - L

The front half goes down the siding and backs out:

C - 6F

The front half couples with the back half:

C - 6F - L - 12F

The train pulls back:

The back half is pushed down the siding and uncouples:

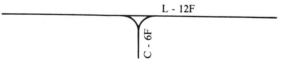

The front half pulls forward, backs down the siding, and recouples:

Figure 25   Solution to the railroad blues.

(3) Notice that it is necessary to do as many couplings as uncouplings, since each uncoupling splits a segment of the train into two pieces, which must then be put back together. Each coupling puts only two pieces together. Let's see that one coupling is not enough. Initially, the locomotive has 19 cars between it and its next destination. Suppose there is one uncoupling. There are three possibilities.

1. The locomotive drives down the siding and then uncouples. It may then back out, in which case their are still six cars between the locomotive and its next destination.
2. The locomotive drives past the siding and then backs down it. There would then still be six cars between the locomotive and its next destination.
3. The locomotive doesn't use the siding. Uncoupling will leave 19 cars between the locomotive and its next destination.

In no case would coupling the remaining cars help.

③ FLIGHTY IDEAS

Yes, it is possible to deliver the packages with only two intermediate stops. Have two groups of eight different cities in the middle of the country. Number the cities 1 to 8 from south to north.

See Figure 26. The two flights from each West Coast airport split the packages among those going to the northern half of the East Coast cities and those going to the southern half.

The flights from the second and third airports refine these splits. The diagram shows that any package can reach any city from any starting city.

Discussion: The solution in the diagram is known as a butterfly network and is one of several networks that would solve this problem, known as Banyan networks. The *Computational Aspects of VLSI* by Jeffrey Ullman (Rockville, MD: Computer Science Press) contains a thorough discussion of these networks.

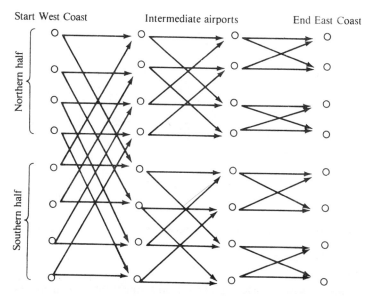

Start West Coast   Intermediate airports   End East Coast

Northern half

Southern half

Figure 26 Airplane flight paths for the Flightly Ideas puzzle. They describe an eight-by-eight Butterfly network.

④ THE ROTARY PROBLEM

The solution is to have five rotaries with four on the outside and one in the middle. Each of the outside rotaries receives 3 of the 12 roads. The inside rotary is connected to each of the outside rotaries by a single road. The danger number is 9 at the worst. (See Figure 27.)

⑤ THE CONTRACT PROBLEM

The lawyers arrive at the following protocol. If at least one side follows the protocol, the lawyers will be able to verify the five conditions.

Amalgamated encodes each of its clear text messages m as follows. First encode m using Behemoth's public encoding key E_b, giving $E_b(m)$. Then use D_a on the result, giving $D_a(E_b(m))$. At this point, Behemoth would be able to reconstruct the clear text

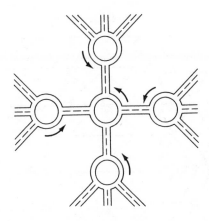

Figure 27 The solution is to have five interconnected rotaries.

m and it would have Amalgamated's signature. Amalgamated then uses the lawyers' public encoding key E_z to get $E_z(D_a(E_b(m)))$. Almagamated sends this out on the public wires. Neither the lawyer nor Behemoth can decrypt it at this point.

The lawyer now retrieves the encoded message and applies D_z, yielding $D_a(E_b(m))$. The lawyer then issues Amalgamated's public key E_a twice, giving $E_a(E_a(D_a(E_b(m)))) = E_a(E_b(m))$.

Behemoth uses a symmetric procedure, sending out $E_z(D_b(E_a(m)))$. The lawyer applies D_z, yielding $D_b(E_a(m))$. Then the lawyer issues E_b twice, giving $E_b(E_b(D_b(E_a(m)))) = E_b(E_a(m))$.

The two results will be equal if and only if the two parties start with the same clear text m and apply their signatures. However, the lawyers don't know what this clear text is. To complete the transaction, the lawyers send $D_b(E_a(m))$ to Amalgamated and $D_a(E_b(m))$ to Behemoth.

Discussion: The connection between codes and computers is long and intimate. Alan Turing, the father of modern computer theory, designed an early computer to break the German Enigma code. For mathematical insights into public key encryption, there are two articles in the *Communications of the Association for Computing Machinery:* D. K. Gifford "Cryptographic Sealing for Information Secrecy and Authentication," vol. 25, no. 4 (April 1982), 274–286, and D. E. Denning, "Digital Signatures with RSA and Other Public-Key Cryptosystems," vol. 27, no. 4 (April 1984), 388–392.

⑥ COMMAND AND CONTROL

(1) Let us number the control stations from 1 to 15, where 1 is the commanding control station. When we say X→Y, we mean that X can send to Y. Here are the connections (See Figure 28):

$1 \to 2, 2 \to 3, 3 \to 4, 3 \to 12, 1 \to 5, 5 \to 6, 6 \to 7, 6 \to 8, 5 \to 9, 9 \to 10, 9 \to 11, 2 \to 13, 13 \to 14$, and $13 \to 15$.

(2) $1 \to 2, 2 \to 3, 3 \to 4, 3 \to 12, 1 \to 5, 5 \to 6, 6 \to 7, 6 \to 8, 5 \to 9, 9 \to 10, 9 \to 11, 2 \to 13, 13 \to 14, 13 \to 15, 4 \to 7, 7 \to 4, 12 \to 8, 8 \to 12, 14 \to 10, 10 \to 14, 15 \to 11, 11 \to 15, 4 \to 1, 12 \to 9, 14 \to 5, 15 \to 6, 7 \to 13, 8 \to 2, 10 \to 3$, and $11 \to 1$.

(3) No; 30 is the minimum possible. With 30 units, every control station receives from two other ones. With fewer, some control station S must receive from just one other control station S'. If S' is incapacitated, then S receives from no one.

⑦ WRONG NUMBER

(1) Any two distinct numbers differ by two digits. Also, any number consists of distinct digits. So transposing any of them must reach a nonworking number.

(2) Many solutions are possible. Here is one. Given a five-digit number $vwxyz$, choose the sixth digit, q, so that the expression $q + 2z + y + 2x + w + 2v$ is divisible by 10. For example, if the number were 42785, the expression $q + 10 + 8 + 14 + 2 + 8 = q + 42$. To obtain a sum that is divisible by 10, q should be 8.

To see why this works, imagine a transposition of $vwxyzq$. Let the transposed digits be d and d'. Then the sum must differ by $|d' - d|$. Since this difference will not be divisible by 10 unless

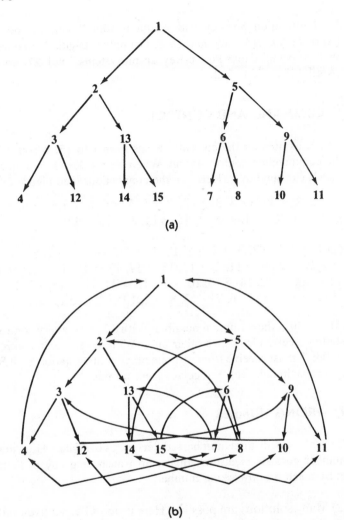

(a)

(b)

Figure 28   The solution to the Command and Control puzzle. (a)
The professor's solution in which the commanding control station
receives nothing from the other control stations. (b) Ecco's
solution tolerates the failure of any single control station. The
connections shown between pairs of bottom-most control stations
are two-way: each station in the pair has a transmitter as well as a
receiver directed toward the other station in the pair.

$d' = d$ (in which case the transposition is harmless), the expression will not be divisible by 10 either, indicating a nonfunctioning number.

⑧ FAKES

Here is how to find the fakes among four coins in three weighings. That will lead to the weights of all 20 coins in 15 weighings. Let the four coins be A, B, C, and D. First weigh A, B, and C. If there are three fakes, the weight will be between 31.8 and 32.1. If there are two fakes and a good one, the weight will be between 32.2 and 32.5. If there is one fake and two good ones, the weight will be between 32.6 and 32.9. If there are only good ones, the weight will be between 33 and 33.3. The point is that you can distinguish the four possibilities. If all three are good or all three are fakes, then you need only weigh D and you will be done in two weighings.

Otherwise, weigh A and D. Then weigh B and D. Each of these weighings tells you that the two coins are both fakes (21.2 to 21.4), one fake and one good (21.6 to 21.8), or two goods (22 to 22.2).

If either pair are both good or both fakes, you can easily determine all the weights. For example, suppose B and D are both good. Then if A and D include one fake, A is the fake. If A, B, and C include two fakes, C is also a fake.

Otherwise, A and D include one good and one fake, and so do B and D. There are two cases. If A, B, and C include two good coins, then D must be fake and A and B must be good. If A, B, and C include two fake coins, then D must be good and A and B must be fake.

CHAPTER SIX

① KNOWLEDGE COORDINATION I

(1) No number of acknowledgments and counteracknowledgments are sufficient. The two generals will never attack. Here is

an argument. Initially, A knows a fact that B doesn't know, and B will only attack when B knows that fact.

Suppose that at some point, one of the two generals, call him general X, knows something that the other one, call him general Y, must know in order to attack. So, X sends a carrier pigeon. Even when Y receives the message, X still cannot attack, because X does not know that Y has received the message. That means that Y knows something, that is that he received the latest message from X, that X must know in order to attack. The argument repeats itself with the roles of X and Y reversed.

(2) One carrier pigeon flight is enough. When the carrier pigeon flies from A to B, the scouts light the beacon. At that point, A knows that B knows that A intends to attack, and B knows that A knows that B knows that A intends to attack, and so on. This state of knowledge and meta-knowledge is what researchers have come to call "common knowledge."

Discussion: Distributed computing systems have been accompanied by an explosion in work on knowledge logic. A branch of this work has been pioneered by J. Halpern and Y. Moses in their article "Knowledge and Common Knowledge in a Distributed Environment," Association for Computing Machinery, Proceedings of the Symposium on Principles of Distributed Computing, Vancouver, B.C., Canada (August 1984), pp. 50–61.

② KNOWLEDGE COORDINATION II

There are three logicians with X's on their backs. In alphabetical order, they are the first, seventh, and tenth.

Here is a proof. The tenth logician figures out that he has an X in the first round. No logician before the tenth has any basis for deciding. The tenth knows that the seventh and first have an X but have not decided. He reasons as follows.

Now, if the Seventh were the last one with an X, the seventh would have been able to decide by using the following reasoning: logician 1 hasn't decided, so he must see another X. I don't see any other X's besides his, so I must have an X.

Since the seventh has not decided, the tenth concludes that

one of the eighth through thirteenth logicians must have an X. The tenth sees no other such logician, so concludes that he must be the one. So, logician 10 says: 'I do have an X on my back and there is at least one other that does, but has not yet realized that he does.' Logicians 11, 12, and 13 retrace the reasoning of logician 10. They decide that they don't have X.

In the second round, none of the first six logicians can decide. But the seventh sees only logician 1 with an X, so he announces, 'I do have an X on my back and there is at least one other that does, but has not yet realized that he does.' Thus, logician 7 is the decider of round 2 that asserts the existence of at least one other X, as required by the problem. The eighth and ninth can decide in round 2 by retracing the reasoning of logician 7.

Logician 1 decides in round 3, since he sees no other X's among the undecided. He announces that there are no others. So, the remaining five among logicians 2 through 6 all decide that they don't have an X.

Notice that if any of the six undecided logicians had an X instead of logician 1, then an additional round would be needed. Since there are only three rounds, we know that logician 1 must have an X.

③ THE COURIERS PROBLEM

(1) Here is one solution out of many:

Courier 1 gets A and B.
Courier 2 gets B and C.
Courier 3 gets C and D.
Courier 4 gets D and E.
Courier 5 gets E and A.
Courier 6 gets A and B.
Courier 7 gets C and D.
Courier 8 gets E.

This works because no two couriers have five distinct parts between them, so the enemy cannot reconstruct the design.

Also, each part P is held by three couriers, so one of the six who gets through must have P.

(2) This solution requires only seven couriers:

Courier 1 gets A, B, and C.
Courier 2 gets C and D.
Courier 3 gets C and D.
Courier 4 gets B and D.
Courier 5 gets B and E.
Courier 6 gets A and E.
Courier 7 gets A and E.

This works because each part is held by three couriers and no two couriers carry all five parts.

(3) If every courier carries no more than two parts, then the original scientist's lower bound shows that there must be at least eight couriers. Furthermore, if any courier has four parts, then some other courier must have the remaining part, but then the two of them would carry all the information. So, in any solution using only six couriers, at least one courier must contain three parts, say A, B, and C. At least three couriers must carry D and at least three must carry E to enable our agent to reconstruct the code. However, no courier may carry both. So, the three couriers carrying D must be different from the three couriers carrying E. Therefore, there must be at least $1 + 3 + 3$ couriers; that is 7.

(4) Use 10 parts A, B, C, D, E, F, G, H, I, and J, distributed among five couriers as follows:

Courier 1 gets A, B, C, D, E, F.
Courier 2 gets A, B, C, G, H, I.
Courier 3 gets A, D, E, H, I, J.
Courier 4 gets B, E, F, G, I, J.
Courier 5 gets C, D, F, G, H, J.

To see that this is correct, note that no one has all of G, H, I, and J, so no single person matches with courier 1. Moreover, no two of couriers 2 through 5 have all of A through F.

④ ROAD WORK

(1) Changing the roads to one way must lengthen trips by two roads in at least some cases. In order for it to be possible to travel from one point to another, there must be some road that is one way toward the plaza and another that is one way away from the plaza. Indeed, these must alternate if neighboring points, for example, C and D, are to be only two roads away from one another.

Now, consider a trip from a point X at the far end of a one-way road pointing away from the plaza to Y at the far end of a one-way road pointing toward the plaza. To get from X to the plaza requires two roads. From the plaza to Y requires two roads for a total of four. Currently, one might drive from X directly to the plaza and then on to Y, for a total of two roads. Provided X and Y are at least four of the circumference roads apart, there is no way to do better.

(2) Figure 29 shows a design that does not lengthen any trip by more than a factor of two. The one-way streets (in the direction

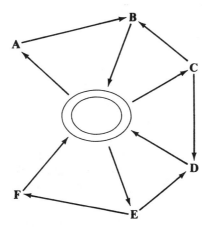

Figure 29 A solution for the Road Work puzzle.

of driving) are as follows: Plaza→, A→B, B→Plaza, Plaza→C, C→B, C→D, D→Plaza, Plaza→E, E→D, E→F, and F→Plaza.

Notice that lengthening the trips by no more than a factor of two is not easy. It is not possible if all of the circumference roads go in the same direction. For example, suppose we laid out the one-way signs as follows: A→B, B→C, C→D, D→E, and E→F along the circumference. Then suppose we had Plaza→A, B→Plaza, Plaza→C, D→Plaza, Plaza→E, and F→Plaza. The trip from C to B would require trips to D, then P, then A, then B.

⑤ COUNTRY ROADS

(1) Since all the roads are the same size, the roads between A, B, and C, between C, B, and D, and between C, D, and E all form equilateral triangles. Since A and D are 170 miles apart, the triangles ABC and DBC are mirror images of one another, with BC as an axis of symmetry. Similarly, BCD and ECD are mirror images, with CD as the axis of symmetry. So, EC and CA are colinear. Hence, A and E are 200 miles apart. The earth is close to Euclidean at these distances.

(2) At least one road is needed. There are four cases, as given in the following list. (We represent the fact that there is a one-way road from X to Y by writing X→Y.)

    1. B→C and D→C. If D→B, then there is no way to go from B to D along two roads. If B→D, then there is no way to go from D to B along two roads.

    2. C→B and C→D. Same problem as in case 1.

    3. B→C and C→D. Because of B→C, B→A is impossible, since there would then be no way to go from A to B along two roads. Hence, A→B and C→A. Similarly, C→D implies that D→E and E→C must hold. But now, there is no way to go from A to E along fewer than four roads, unless B→D holds. But then there is no way to go from D to B along fewer than four roads.

    4. C→B and D→C. Since the figure is symmetric about the

perpendicular bisector from C to DB, a very similar argument shows that this case does not work either.

(3) Only 100 miles of road building is needed. Simply build a road parallel to the one between B and D. Then, one solution is to direct the roads as follows: A→B, B→D, D→B, D→E, E→C, C→A, C→D, B→C.

⑥ SUBWAY LAYOUT

(1) One of the best solutions is to use the routes between 1 and 4, 2 and 5, 3 and 7, 4 and 5, 5 and 7, 5 and 8, and 6 and 8. This would cost 72 billion pesos.

(2) Order the routes from the cheapest to the most expensive. The first few are shown in the table on this page.
 Now take each route in turn and see if it connects two points that are not yet connected. The first one connects 5 and 8. Since no routes have yet been included, include that route. Similarly, include routes between 1 and 4, 3 and 7, 5 and 7, and 2 and 5. Now we come to the route between 2 and 7. Since the routes we already have include a route between 2 and 5 and 5 and 7, we don't need that one. We do include the routes between 4 and 5 and between 6 and 8, however. With that, we are done. When adding any route, we've made sure that no cheaper way of connecting two unconnected points was possible, so this method is guaranteed to give a minimum cost.

The first 12 lowest-cost routes

Point	Point	Cost	Point	Point	Cost
5	8	9	4	5	11
1	4	10	6	8	11
3	7	10	3	8	12
5	7	10	2	6	13
2	5	11	3	5	13
2	7	11	4	6	13

Ecco's routes selected to guarantee
travel times of no more than five
minutes to and from station 1

Point	Point	Cost	Time
1	4	10	2
1	8	14	2
4	6	13	2
3	4	14	1
7	8	15	3
2	8	16	2
5	8	9	1

(3) The table on this page shows Ecco's solution. Note that it is possible to go between 1 and any point in five minutes or less of travel time.

Discussion: These solutions are inspired by the minimum spanning tree and shortest path algorithms. *Data Structures and Algorithms* by Al Aho, John Hopcroft, and Jeff Ullman. (Reading, MA: Addison-Wesley) discusses the implementation of these algorithms on computers.

CHAPTER SEVEN

① PUZZLE-MAD KIDNAPPER

(1) If you know the binary number system, just consider the binary representation. Each bit is a coin. If you don't, then observe the following. Any number between 1 and 2000 can be represented as the sum of 11 numbers, each of which can take only two values. The first number is either 1028 or 0. The second: 512 or 0. The third: 256 or 0. The fourth: 128 or 0. The fifth: 64 or 0. The sixth: 32 or 0. The seventh: 16 or 0. The eighth: 8 or 0. The ninth: 4 or 0. The tenth: 2 or 0. The eleventh: 1 or 0. Without lying, the questions then take the following form.

Is the number 1028 or greater? Is the number either between 512 and 1027, or between 1540 and 2000? They continue getting increasingly complicated. Although the last one is simple enough: Is the number even?

(2) One can solve the coin problem in 33 questions by asking three times about each coin and taking the majority value.

(3) To solve the coin problem in 23 questions when each question is answered immediately: ask two questions about the first coin; if they are consistent, then ask two questions about the second coin, and so on. Whenever the two questions are answered inconsistently, ask a third question and take the majority. This may require 10 sets of two questions and one set of three questions.

(4) To solve the coin problem in 15 questions where the respondent answers all the questions at the end, ask them in the following way.

1. Is the first coin heads?
2. Is the second coin heads?

And so on, until:

11. Is the eleventh coin heads?

12. Were you telling the truth about coins 1 through 7? (Equivalently, you could ask whether there are an odd number of heads in coins 1 through 7. If the answer is consistent with the responses given in the first seven answers, then the answer to 12 is yes, otherwise, no.)

13. Were you telling the truth in your first 10 answers about coins 1 through 4 and about coins 8, 9, 10?

14. Were you telling the truth in your first 11 answers about coins 1, 2, 5, 6, 8, 9, and 11?

15. Were you telling the truth in your first 11 answers about coins 1, 3, 5, 7, 8, 10, 11?

Refer to the table to decide which of the 15 answers, if any, was a lie. This table tabulates the answer to each question and gives the conclusion that is then possible. Any "yes" to one of the last four questions confirms the orientations of the coins that the question refers to. If only zero or one of the last four questions is answered "no," then the first 11 answers were truthful and the "no" is a lie.

Discussion: S. M. Ulam, in his delightful book *The Adventures of a Mathematician* (New York: Charles Scribner and Sons), poses a similar problem, challenging his readers to solve it. Congratulations.

Discovering the lie in Baskerhound's first 11 answers

Answer to question 12	Answer to question 13	Answer to question 14	Answer to question 15	Question answered falsely
yes	yes	yes	yes	none
yes	yes	yes	no	fifteen
yes	yes	no	yes	fourteen
yes	yes	no	no	eleven
yes	no	yes	yes	thirteen
yes	no	yes	no	ten
yes	no	no	yes	nine
yes	no	no	no	eight
no	yes	yes	yes	twelve
no	yes	yes	no	seven
no	yes	no	yes	six
no	yes	no	no	five
no	no	yes	yes	four
no	no	yes	no	three
no	no	no	yes	two
no	no	no	no	one

② MYSTERY

Here are the decoded sentences. Evangeline thinks there is a
hint in the structure of the code.

> very clever aren't you?
>
> we need your help, alone.
>
> everyone knows we are adversaries. in truth, we are
> friends. we will get you, dr. ecco.

A CATALOG OF SELECTED
DOVER BOOKS
IN ALL FIELDS OF INTEREST

A CATALOG OF SELECTED DOVER
BOOKS IN ALL FIELDS OF INTEREST

CONCERNING THE SPIRITUAL IN ART, Wassily Kandinsky. Pioneering work by father of abstract art. Thoughts on color theory, nature of art. Analysis of earlier masters. 12 illustrations. 80pp. of text. 5⅜ x 8½. 0-486-23411-8

CELTIC ART: The Methods of Construction, George Bain. Simple geometric techniques for making Celtic interlacements, spirals, Kells-type initials, animals, humans, etc. Over 500 illustrations. 160pp. 9 x 12. (Available in U.S. only.) 0-486-22923-8

AN ATLAS OF ANATOMY FOR ARTISTS, Fritz Schider. Most thorough reference work on art anatomy in the world. Hundreds of illustrations, including selections from works by Vesalius, Leonardo, Goya, Ingres, Michelangelo, others. 593 illustrations. 192pp. 7⅛ x 10¼. 0-486-20241-0

CELTIC HAND STROKE-BY-STROKE (Irish Half-Uncial from "The Book of Kells"): An Arthur Baker Calligraphy Manual, Arthur Baker. Complete guide to creating each letter of the alphabet in distinctive Celtic manner. Covers hand position, strokes, pens, inks, paper, more. Illustrated. 48pp. 8¼ x 11. 0-486-24336-2

EASY ORIGAMI, John Montroll. Charming collection of 32 projects (hat, cup, pelican, piano, swan, many more) specially designed for the novice origami hobbyist. Clearly illustrated easy-to-follow instructions insure that even beginning papercrafters will achieve successful results. 48pp. 8¼ x 11. 0-486-27298-2

BLOOMINGDALE'S ILLUSTRATED 1886 CATALOG: Fashions, Dry Goods and Housewares, Bloomingdale Brothers. Famed merchants' extremely rare catalog depicting about 1,700 products: clothing, housewares, firearms, dry goods, jewelry, more. Invaluable for dating, identifying vintage items. Also, copyright-free graphics for artists, designers. Co-published with Henry Ford Museum & Greenfield Village. 160pp. 8¼ x 11. 0-486-25780-0

THE ART OF WORLDLY WISDOM, Baltasar Gracian. "Think with the few and speak with the many," "Friends are a second existence," and "Be able to forget" are among this 1637 volume's 300 pithy maxims. A perfect source of mental and spiritual refreshment, it can be opened at random and appreciated either in brief or at length. 128pp. 5⅜ x 8½. 0-486-44034-6

JOHNSON'S DICTIONARY: A Modern Selection, Samuel Johnson (E. L. McAdam and George Milne, eds.). This modern version reduces the original 1755 edition's 2,300 pages of definitions and literary examples to a more manageable length, retaining the verbal pleasure and historical curiosity of the original. 480pp. 5⁵⁄₁₆ x 8¼. 0-486-44089-3

ADVENTURES OF HUCKLEBERRY FINN, Mark Twain, Illustrated by E. W. Kemble. A work of eternal richness and complexity, a source of ongoing critical debate, and a literary landmark, Twain's 1885 masterpiece about a barefoot boy's journey of self-discovery has enthralled readers around the world. This handsome clothbound reproduction of the first edition features all 174 of the original black-and-white illustrations. 368pp. 5⅜ x 8½. 0-486-44322-1

STICKLEY CRAFTSMAN FURNITURE CATALOGS, Gustav Stickley and L. & J. G. Stickley. Beautiful, functional furniture in two authentic catalogs from 1910. 594 illustrations, including 277 photos, show settles, rockers, armchairs, reclining chairs, bookcases, desks, tables. 183pp. 6½ x 9¼.   0-486-23838-5

AMERICAN LOCOMOTIVES IN HISTORIC PHOTOGRAPHS: 1858 to 1949, Ron Ziel (ed.). A rare collection of 126 meticulously detailed official photographs, called "builder portraits," of American locomotives that majestically chronicle the rise of steam locomotive power in America. Introduction. Detailed captions. xi+ 129pp. 9 x 12.   0-486-27393-8

AMERICA'S LIGHTHOUSES: An Illustrated History, Francis Ross Holland, Jr. Delightfully written, profusely illustrated fact-filled survey of over 200 American lighthouses since 1716. History, anecdotes, technological advances, more. 240pp. 8 x 10¾.
0-486-25576-X

TOWARDS A NEW ARCHITECTURE, Le Corbusier. Pioneering manifesto by founder of "International School." Technical and aesthetic theories, views of industry, economics, relation of form to function, "mass-production split" and much more. Profusely illustrated. 320pp. 6⅛ x 9¼. (Available in U.S. only.)   0-486-25023-7

HOW THE OTHER HALF LIVES, Jacob Riis. Famous journalistic record, exposing poverty and degradation of New York slums around 1900, by major social reformer. 100 striking and influential photographs. 233pp. 10 x 7⅞.   0-486-22012-5

FRUIT KEY AND TWIG KEY TO TREES AND SHRUBS, William M. Harlow. One of the handiest and most widely used identification aids. Fruit key covers 120 deciduous and evergreen species; twig key 160 deciduous species. Easily used. Over 300 photographs. 126pp. 5⅜ x 8½.   0-486-20511-8

COMMON BIRD SONGS, Dr. Donald J. Borror. Songs of 60 most common U.S. birds: robins, sparrows, cardinals, bluejays, finches, more—arranged in order of increasing complexity. Up to 9 variations of songs of each species.
Cassette and manual 0-486-99911-4

ORCHIDS AS HOUSE PLANTS, Rebecca Tyson Northen. Grow cattleyas and many other kinds of orchids—in a window, in a case, or under artificial light. 63 illustrations. 148pp. 5⅜ x 8½.   0-486-23261-1

MONSTER MAZES, Dave Phillips. Masterful mazes at four levels of difficulty. Avoid deadly perils and evil creatures to find magical treasures. Solutions for all 32 exciting illustrated puzzles. 48pp. 8¼ x 11.   0-486-26005-4

MOZART'S DON GIOVANNI (DOVER OPERA LIBRETTO SERIES), Wolfgang Amadeus Mozart. Introduced and translated by Ellen H. Bleiler. Standard Italian libretto, with complete English translation. Convenient and thoroughly portable—an ideal companion for reading along with a recording or the performance itself. Introduction. List of characters. Plot summary. 121pp. 5¼ x 8½. 0-486-24944-1

FRANK LLOYD WRIGHT'S DANA HOUSE, Donald Hoffmann. Pictorial essay of residential masterpiece with over 160 interior and exterior photos, plans, elevations, sketches and studies. 128pp. 9¼ x 10¾.   0-486-29120-0

THE CLARINET AND CLARINET PLAYING, David Pino. Lively, comprehensive work features suggestions about technique, musicianship, and musical interpretation, as well as guidelines for teaching, making your own reeds, and preparing for public performance. Includes an intriguing look at clarinet history. "A godsend," *The Clarinet,* Journal of the International Clarinet Society. Appendixes. 7 illus. 320pp. 5⅜ x 8½. 0-486-40270-3

HOLLYWOOD GLAMOR PORTRAITS, John Kobal (ed.). 145 photos from 1926-49. Harlow, Gable, Bogart, Bacall; 94 stars in all. Full background on photographers, technical aspects. 160pp. 8⅜ x 11¼. 0-486-23352-9

THE RAVEN AND OTHER FAVORITE POEMS, Edgar Allan Poe. Over 40 of the author's most memorable poems: "The Bells," "Ulalume," "Israfel," "To Helen," "The Conqueror Worm," "Eldorado," "Annabel Lee," many more. Alphabetic lists of titles and first lines. 64pp. $5\frac{3}{16}$ x 8¼. 0-486-26685-0

PERSONAL MEMOIRS OF U. S. GRANT, Ulysses Simpson Grant. Intelligent, deeply moving firsthand account of Civil War campaigns, considered by many the finest military memoirs ever written. Includes letters, historic photographs, maps and more. 528pp. 6⅛ x 9¼. 0-486-28587-1

ANCIENT EGYPTIAN MATERIALS AND INDUSTRIES, A. Lucas and J. Harris. Fascinating, comprehensive, thoroughly documented text describes this ancient civilization's vast resources and the processes that incorporated them in daily life, including the use of animal products, building materials, cosmetics, perfumes and incense, fibers, glazed ware, glass and its manufacture, materials used in the mummification process, and much more. 544pp. 6⅛ x 9¼. (Available in U.S. only.) 0-486-40446-3

RUSSIAN STORIES/RUSSKIE RASSKAZY: A Dual-Language Book, edited by Gleb Struve. Twelve tales by such masters as Chekhov, Tolstoy, Dostoevsky, Pushkin, others. Excellent word-for-word English translations on facing pages, plus teaching and study aids, Russian/English vocabulary, biographical/critical introductions, more. 416pp. 5⅜ x 8½. 0-486-26244-8

PHILADELPHIA THEN AND NOW: 60 Sites Photographed in the Past and Present, Kenneth Finkel and Susan Oyama. Rare photographs of City Hall, Logan Square, Independence Hall, Betsy Ross House, other landmarks juxtaposed with contemporary views. Captures changing face of historic city. Introduction. Captions. 128pp. 8¼ x 11. 0-486-25790-8

NORTH AMERICAN INDIAN LIFE: Customs and Traditions of 23 Tribes, Elsie Clews Parsons (ed.). 27 fictionalized essays by noted anthropologists examine religion, customs, government, additional facets of life among the Winnebago, Crow, Zuni, Eskimo, other tribes. 480pp. 6⅛ x 9¼. 0-486-27377-6

TECHNICAL MANUAL AND DICTIONARY OF CLASSICAL BALLET, Gail Grant. Defines, explains, comments on steps, movements, poses and concepts. 15-page pictorial section. Basic book for student, viewer. 127pp. 5⅜ x 8½. 0-486-21843-0

THE MALE AND FEMALE FIGURE IN MOTION: 60 Classic Photographic Sequences, Eadweard Muybridge. 60 true-action photographs of men and women walking, running, climbing, bending, turning, etc., reproduced from rare 19th-century masterpiece. vi + 121pp. 9 x 12. 0-486-24745-7

ANIMALS: 1,419 Copyright-Free Illustrations of Mammals, Birds, Fish, Insects, etc., Jim Harter (ed.). Clear wood engravings present, in extremely lifelike poses, over 1,000 species of animals. One of the most extensive pictorial sourcebooks of its kind. Captions. Index. 284pp. 9 x 12. 0-486-23766-4

1001 QUESTIONS ANSWERED ABOUT THE SEASHORE, N. J. Berrill and Jacquelyn Berrill. Queries answered about dolphins, sea snails, sponges, starfish, fishes, shore birds, many others. Covers appearance, breeding, growth, feeding, much more. 305pp. 5¼ x 8¼. 0-486-23366-9

ATTRACTING BIRDS TO YOUR YARD, William J. Weber. Easy-to-follow guide offers advice on how to attract the greatest diversity of birds: birdhouses, feeders, water and waterers, much more. 96pp. 5³/₁₆ x 8¼. 0-486-28927-3

MEDICINAL AND OTHER USES OF NORTH AMERICAN PLANTS: A Historical Survey with Special Reference to the Eastern Indian Tribes, Charlotte Erichsen-Brown. Chronological historical citations document 500 years of usage of plants, trees, shrubs native to eastern Canada, northeastern U.S. Also complete identifying information. 343 illustrations. 544pp. 6½ x 9¼. 0-486-25951-X

STORYBOOK MAZES, Dave Phillips. 23 stories and mazes on two-page spreads: Wizard of Oz, Treasure Island, Robin Hood, etc. Solutions. 64pp. 8¼ x 11. 0-486-23628-5

AMERICAN NEGRO SONGS: 230 Folk Songs and Spirituals, Religious and Secular, John W. Work. This authoritative study traces the African influences of songs sung and played by black Americans at work, in church, and as entertainment. The author discusses the lyric significance of such songs as "Swing Low, Sweet Chariot," "John Henry," and others and offers the words and music for 230 songs. Bibliography. Index of Song Titles. 272pp. 6½ x 9¼. 0-486-40271-1

MOVIE-STAR PORTRAITS OF THE FORTIES, John Kobal (ed.). 163 glamor, studio photos of 106 stars of the 1940s: Rita Hayworth, Ava Gardner, Marlon Brando, Clark Gable, many more. 176pp. 8⅜ x 11¼. 0-486-23546-7

YEKL and THE IMPORTED BRIDEGROOM AND OTHER STORIES OF YIDDISH NEW YORK, Abraham Cahan. Film Hester Street based on *Yekl* (1896). Novel, other stories among first about Jewish immigrants on N.Y.'s East Side. 240pp. 5⅜ x 8½. 0-486-22427-9

SELECTED POEMS, Walt Whitman. Generous sampling from *Leaves of Grass*. Twenty-four poems include "I Hear America Singing," "Song of the Open Road," "I Sing the Body Electric," "When Lilacs Last in the Dooryard Bloom'd," "O Captain! My Captain!"–all reprinted from an authoritative edition. Lists of titles and first lines. 128pp. 5³/₁₆ x 8¼. 0-486-26878-0

SONGS OF EXPERIENCE: Facsimile Reproduction with 26 Plates in Full Color, William Blake. 26 full-color plates from a rare 1826 edition. Includes "The Tyger," "London," "Holy Thursday," and other poems. Printed text of poems. 48pp. 5¼ x 7. 0-486-24636-1

THE BEST TALES OF HOFFMANN, E. T. A. Hoffmann. 10 of Hoffmann's most important stories: "Nutcracker and the King of Mice," "The Golden Flowerpot," etc. 458pp. 5⅜ x 8½. 0-486-21793-0

THE BOOK OF TEA, Kakuzo Okakura. Minor classic of the Orient: entertaining, charming explanation, interpretation of traditional Japanese culture in terms of tea ceremony. 94pp. 5⅜ x 8½. 0-486-20070-1

FRENCH STORIES/CONTES FRANÇAIS: A Dual-Language Book, Wallace Fowlie. Ten stories by French masters, Voltaire to Camus: "Micromegas" by Voltaire; "The Atheist's Mass" by Balzac; "Minuet" by de Maupassant; "The Guest" by Camus, six more. Excellent English translations on facing pages. Also French-English vocabulary list, exercises, more. 352pp. 5⅜ x 8½.　　　　　0-486-26443-2

CHICAGO AT THE TURN OF THE CENTURY IN PHOTOGRAPHS: 122 Historic Views from the Collections of the Chicago Historical Society, Larry A. Viskochil. Rare large-format prints offer detailed views of City Hall, State Street, the Loop, Hull House, Union Station, many other landmarks, circa 1904-1913. Introduction. Captions. Maps. 144pp. 9⅜ x 12¼.　　　　　0-486-24656-6

OLD BROOKLYN IN EARLY PHOTOGRAPHS, 1865-1929, William Lee Younger. Luna Park, Gravesend race track, construction of Grand Army Plaza, moving of Hotel Brighton, etc. 157 previously unpublished photographs. 165pp. 8⅞ x 11¾.
　　　　　0-486-23587-4

THE MYTHS OF THE NORTH AMERICAN INDIANS, Lewis Spence. Rich anthology of the myths and legends of the Algonquins, Iroquois, Pawnees and Sioux, prefaced by an extensive historical and ethnological commentary. 36 illustrations. 480pp. 5⅜ x 8½.　　　　　0-486-25967-6

AN ENCYCLOPEDIA OF BATTLES: Accounts of Over 1,560 Battles from 1479 B.C. to the Present, David Eggenberger. Essential details of every major battle in recorded history from the first battle of Megiddo in 1479 B.C. to Grenada in 1984. List of Battle Maps. New Appendix covering the years 1967-1984. Index. 99 illustrations. 544pp. 6½ x 9¼.　　　　　0-486-24913-1

SAILING ALONE AROUND THE WORLD, Captain Joshua Slocum. First man to sail around the world, alone, in small boat. One of great feats of seamanship told in delightful manner. 67 illustrations. 294pp. 5⅜ x 8½.　　　　　0-486-20326-3

ANARCHISM AND OTHER ESSAYS, Emma Goldman. Powerful, penetrating, prophetic essays on direct action, role of minorities, prison reform, puritan hypocrisy, violence, etc. 271pp. 5⅜ x 8½.　　　　　0-486-22484-8

MYTHS OF THE HINDUS AND BUDDHISTS, Ananda K. Coomaraswamy and Sister Nivedita. Great stories of the epics; deeds of Krishna, Shiva, taken from puranas, Vedas, folk tales; etc. 32 illustrations. 400pp. 5⅜ x 8½.　　　　　0-486-21759-0

MY BONDAGE AND MY FREEDOM, Frederick Douglass. Born a slave, Douglass became outspoken force in antislavery movement. The best of Douglass' autobiographies. Graphic description of slave life. 464pp. 5⅜ x 8½.　　0-486-22457-0

FOLLOWING THE EQUATOR: A Journey Around the World, Mark Twain. Fascinating humorous account of 1897 voyage to Hawaii, Australia, India, New Zealand, etc. Ironic, bemused reports on peoples, customs, climate, flora and fauna, politics, much more. 197 illustrations. 720pp. 5⅜ x 8½.　　　　　0-486-26113-1

THE PEOPLE CALLED SHAKERS, Edward D. Andrews. Definitive study of Shakers: origins, beliefs, practices, dances, social organization, furniture and crafts, etc. 33 illustrations. 351pp. 5⅜ x 8½.　　　　　0-486-21081-2

THE MYTHS OF GREECE AND ROME, H. A. Guerber. A classic of mythology, generously illustrated, long prized for its simple, graphic, accurate retelling of the principal myths of Greece and Rome, and for its commentary on their origins and significance. With 64 illustrations by Michelangelo, Raphael, Titian, Rubens, Canova, Bernini and others. 480pp. 5⅜ x 8½.　　　　　0-486-27584-1

PSYCHOLOGY OF MUSIC, Carl E. Seashore. Classic work discusses music as a medium from psychological viewpoint. Clear treatment of physical acoustics, auditory apparatus, sound perception, development of musical skills, nature of musical feeling, host of other topics. 88 figures. 408pp. 5⅜ x 8½. 0-486-21851-1

LIFE IN ANCIENT EGYPT, Adolf Erman. Fullest, most thorough, detailed older account with much not in more recent books, domestic life, religion, magic, medicine, commerce, much more. Many illustrations reproduce tomb paintings, carvings, hieroglyphs, etc. 597pp. 5⅜ x 8½. 0-486-22632-8

SUNDIALS, Their Theory and Construction, Albert Waugh. Far and away the best, most thorough coverage of ideas, mathematics concerned, types, construction, adjusting anywhere. Simple, nontechnical treatment allows even children to build several of these dials. Over 100 illustrations. 230pp. 5⅜ x 8½. 0-486-22947-5

THEORETICAL HYDRODYNAMICS, L. M. Milne-Thomson. Classic exposition of the mathematical theory of fluid motion, applicable to both hydrodynamics and aerodynamics. Over 600 exercises. 768pp. 6⅛ x 9¼. 0-486-68970-0

OLD-TIME VIGNETTES IN FULL COLOR, Carol Belanger Grafton (ed.). Over 390 charming, often sentimental illustrations, selected from archives of Victorian graphics–pretty women posing, children playing, food, flowers, kittens and puppies, smiling cherubs, birds and butterflies, much more. All copyright-free. 48pp. 9¼ x 12¼. 0-486-27269-9

PERSPECTIVE FOR ARTISTS, Rex Vicat Cole. Depth, perspective of sky and sea, shadows, much more, not usually covered. 391 diagrams, 81 reproductions of drawings and paintings. 279pp. 5⅜ x 8½. 0-486-22487-2

DRAWING THE LIVING FIGURE, Joseph Sheppard. Innovative approach to artistic anatomy focuses on specifics of surface anatomy, rather than muscles and bones. Over 170 drawings of live models in front, back and side views, and in widely varying poses. Accompanying diagrams. 177 illustrations. Introduction. Index. 144pp. 8⅜ x11¼. 0-486-26723-7

GOTHIC AND OLD ENGLISH ALPHABETS: 100 Complete Fonts, Dan X. Solo. Add power, elegance to posters, signs, other graphics with 100 stunning copyright-free alphabets: Blackstone, Dolbey, Germania, 97 more–including many lower-case, numerals, punctuation marks. 104pp. 8⅛ x 11. 0-486-24695-7

THE BOOK OF WOOD CARVING, Charles Marshall Sayers. Finest book for beginners discusses fundamentals and offers 34 designs. "Absolutely first rate . . . well thought out and well executed."–E. J. Tangerman. 118pp. 7¾ x 10⅝. 0-486-23654-4

ILLUSTRATED CATALOG OF CIVIL WAR MILITARY GOODS: Union Army Weapons, Insignia, Uniform Accessories, and Other Equipment, Schuyler, Hartley, and Graham. Rare, profusely illustrated 1846 catalog includes Union Army uniform and dress regulations, arms and ammunition, coats, insignia, flags, swords, rifles, etc. 226 illustrations. 160pp. 9 x 12. 0-486-24939-5

WOMEN'S FASHIONS OF THE EARLY 1900s: An Unabridged Republication of "New York Fashions, 1909," National Cloak & Suit Co. Rare catalog of mail-order fashions documents women's and children's clothing styles shortly after the turn of the century. Captions offer full descriptions, prices. Invaluable resource for fashion, costume historians. Approximately 725 illustrations. 128pp. 8⅜ x 11¼. 0-486-27276-1

HOW TO DO BEADWORK, Mary White. Fundamental book on craft from simple projects to five-bead chains and woven works. 106 illustrations. 142pp. 5⅜ x 8.
0-486-20697-1

THE 1912 AND 1915 GUSTAV STICKLEY FURNITURE CATALOGS, Gustav Stickley. With over 200 detailed illustrations and descriptions, these two catalogs are essential reading and reference materials and identification guides for Stickley furniture. Captions cite materials, dimensions and prices. 112pp. 6½ x 9¼. 0-486-26676-1

EARLY AMERICAN LOCOMOTIVES, John H. White, Jr. Finest locomotive engravings from early 19th century: historical (1804–74), main-line (after 1870), special, foreign, etc. 147 plates. 142pp. 11⅜ x 8¼. 0-486-22772-3

LITTLE BOOK OF EARLY AMERICAN CRAFTS AND TRADES, Peter Stockham (ed.). 1807 children's book explains crafts and trades: baker, hatter, cooper, potter, and many others. 23 copperplate illustrations. 140pp. 4⅝ x 6.
0-486-23336-7

VICTORIAN FASHIONS AND COSTUMES FROM HARPER'S BAZAR, 1867–1898, Stella Blum (ed.). Day costumes, evening wear, sports clothes, shoes, hats, other accessories in over 1,000 detailed engravings. 320pp. 9⅜ x 12¼.
0-486-22990-4

THE LONG ISLAND RAIL ROAD IN EARLY PHOTOGRAPHS, Ron Ziel. Over 220 rare photos, informative text document origin (1844) and development of rail service on Long Island. Vintage views of early trains, locomotives, stations, passengers, crews, much more. Captions. 8⅞ x 11¾. 0-486-26301-0

VOYAGE OF THE LIBERDADE, Joshua Slocum. Great 19th-century mariner's thrilling, first-hand account of the wreck of his ship off South America, the 35-foot boat he built from the wreckage, and its remarkable voyage home. 128pp. 5⅜ x 8½.
0-486-40022-0

TEN BOOKS ON ARCHITECTURE, Vitruvius. The most important book ever written on architecture. Early Roman aesthetics, technology, classical orders, site selection, all other aspects. Morgan translation. 331pp. 5⅜ x 8½. 0-486-20645-9

THE HUMAN FIGURE IN MOTION, Eadweard Muybridge. More than 4,500 stopped-action photos, in action series, showing undraped men, women, children jumping, lying down, throwing, sitting, wrestling, carrying, etc. 390pp. 7⅞ x 10⅝.
0-486-20204-6 Clothbd.

TREES OF THE EASTERN AND CENTRAL UNITED STATES AND CANADA, William M. Harlow. Best one-volume guide to 140 trees. Full descriptions, woodlore, range, etc. Over 600 illustrations. Handy size. 288pp. 4½ x 6⅜. 0-486-20395-6

GROWING AND USING HERBS AND SPICES, Milo Miloradovich. Versatile handbook provides all the information needed for cultivation and use of all the herbs and spices available in North America. 4 illustrations. Index. Glossary. 236pp. 5⅜ x 8½.
0-486-25058-X

BIG BOOK OF MAZES AND LABYRINTHS, Walter Shepherd. 50 mazes and labyrinths in all–classical, solid, ripple, and more–in one great volume. Perfect inexpensive puzzler for clever youngsters. Full solutions. 112pp. 8⅛ x 11. 0-486-22951-3

PIANO TUNING, J. Cree Fischer. Clearest, best book for beginner, amateur. Simple repairs, raising dropped notes, tuning by easy method of flattened fifths. No previous skills needed. 4 illustrations. 201pp. 5⅜ x 8½. 0-486-23267-0

HINTS TO SINGERS, Lillian Nordica. Selecting the right teacher, developing confidence, overcoming stage fright, and many other important skills receive thoughtful discussion in this indispensible guide, written by a world-famous diva of four decades' experience. 96pp. 5⅜ x 8½. 0-486-40094-8

THE COMPLETE NONSENSE OF EDWARD LEAR, Edward Lear. All nonsense limericks, zany alphabets, Owl and Pussycat, songs, nonsense botany, etc., illustrated by Lear. Total of 320pp. 5⅜ x 8½. (Available in U.S. only.) 0-486-20167-8

VICTORIAN PARLOUR POETRY: An Annotated Anthology, Michael R. Turner. 117 gems by Longfellow, Tennyson, Browning, many lesser-known poets. "The Village Blacksmith," "Curfew Must Not Ring Tonight," "Only a Baby Small," dozens more, often difficult to find elsewhere. Index of poets, titles, first lines. xxiii + 325pp. 5⅝ x 8¼. 0-486-27044-0

DUBLINERS, James Joyce. Fifteen stories offer vivid, tightly focused observations of the lives of Dublin's poorer classes. At least one, "The Dead," is considered a masterpiece. Reprinted complete and unabridged from standard edition. 160pp. 5 3/16 x 8¼. 0-486-26870-5

GREAT WEIRD TALES: 14 Stories by Lovecraft, Blackwood, Machen and Others, S. T. Joshi (ed.). 14 spellbinding tales, including "The Sin Eater," by Fiona McLeod, "The Eye Above the Mantel," by Frank Belknap Long, as well as renowned works by R. H. Barlow, Lord Dunsany, Arthur Machen, W. C. Morrow and eight other masters of the genre. 256pp. 5⅜ x 8½. (Available in U.S. only.) 0-486-40436-6

THE BOOK OF THE SACRED MAGIC OF ABRAMELIN THE MAGE, translated by S. MacGregor Mathers. Medieval manuscript of ceremonial magic. Basic document in Aleister Crowley, Golden Dawn groups. 268pp. 5⅜ x 8½. 0-486-23211-5

THE BATTLES THAT CHANGED HISTORY, Fletcher Pratt. Eminent historian profiles 16 crucial conflicts, ancient to modern, that changed the course of civilization. 352pp. 5⅜ x 8½. 0-486-41129-X

NEW RUSSIAN-ENGLISH AND ENGLISH-RUSSIAN DICTIONARY, M. A. O'Brien. This is a remarkably handy Russian dictionary, containing a surprising amount of information, including over 70,000 entries. 366pp. 4½ x 6⅛. 0-486-20208-9

NEW YORK IN THE FORTIES, Andreas Feininger. 162 brilliant photographs by the well-known photographer, formerly with *Life* magazine. Commuters, shoppers, Times Square at night, much else from city at its peak. Captions by John von Hartz. 181pp. 9¼ x 10¾. 0-486-23585-8

INDIAN SIGN LANGUAGE, William Tomkins. Over 525 signs developed by Sioux and other tribes. Written instructions and diagrams. Also 290 pictographs. 111pp. 6⅛ x 9¼. 0-486-22029-X

ANATOMY: A Complete Guide for Artists, Joseph Sheppard. A master of figure drawing shows artists how to render human anatomy convincingly. Over 460 illustrations. 224pp. 8⅜ x 11¼. 0-486-27279-6

MEDIEVAL CALLIGRAPHY: Its History and Technique, Marc Drogin. Spirited history, comprehensive instruction manual covers 13 styles (ca. 4th century through 15th). Excellent photographs; directions for duplicating medieval techniques with modern tools. 224pp. 8⅜ x 11¼. 0-486-26142-5

DRIED FLOWERS: How to Prepare Them, Sarah Whitlock and Martha Rankin. Complete instructions on how to use silica gel, meal and borax, perlite aggregate, sand and borax, glycerine and water to create attractive permanent flower arrangements. 12 illustrations. 32pp. 5⅜ x 8½. 0-486-21802-3

EASY-TO-MAKE BIRD FEEDERS FOR WOODWORKERS, Scott D. Campbell. Detailed, simple-to-use guide for designing, constructing, caring for and using feeders. Text, illustrations for 12 classic and contemporary designs. 96pp. 5⅜ x 8½. 0-486-25847-5

THE COMPLETE BOOK OF BIRDHOUSE CONSTRUCTION FOR WOOD-WORKERS, Scott D. Campbell. Detailed instructions, illustrations, tables. Also data on bird habitat and instinct patterns. Bibliography. 3 tables. 63 illustrations in 15 figures. 48pp. 5¼ x 8½. 0-486-24407-5

SCOTTISH WONDER TALES FROM MYTH AND LEGEND, Donald A. Mackenzie. 16 lively tales tell of giants rumbling down mountainsides, of a magic wand that turns stone pillars into warriors, of gods and goddesses, evil hags, powerful forces and more. 240pp. 5⅜ x 8½. 0-486-29677-6

THE HISTORY OF UNDERCLOTHES, C. Willett Cunnington and Phyllis Cunnington. Fascinating, well-documented survey covering six centuries of English undergarments, enhanced with over 100 illustrations: 12th-century laced-up bodice, footed long drawers (1795), 19th-century bustles, 19th-century corsets for men, Victorian "bust improvers," much more. 272pp. 5⅜ x 8¼. 0-486-27124-2

ARTS AND CRAFTS FURNITURE: The Complete Brooks Catalog of 1912, Brooks Manufacturing Co. Photos and detailed descriptions of more than 150 now very collectible furniture designs from the Arts and Crafts movement depict davenports, settees, buffets, desks, tables, chairs, bedsteads, dressers and more, all built of solid, quarter-sawed oak. Invaluable for students and enthusiasts of antiques, Americana and the decorative arts. 80pp. 6½ x 9¼. 0-486-27471-3

WILBUR AND ORVILLE: A Biography of the Wright Brothers, Fred Howard. Definitive, crisply written study tells the full story of the brothers' lives and work. A vividly written biography, unparalleled in scope and color, that also captures the spirit of an extraordinary era. 560pp. 6⅛ x 9¼. 0-486-40297-5

THE ARTS OF THE SAILOR: Knotting, Splicing and Ropework, Hervey Garrett Smith. Indispensable shipboard reference covers tools, basic knots and useful hitches; handsewing and canvas work, more. Over 100 illustrations. Delightful reading for sea lovers. 256pp. 5⅜ x 8½. 0-486-26440-8

FRANK LLOYD WRIGHT'S FALLINGWATER: The House and Its History, Second, Revised Edition, Donald Hoffmann. A total revision–both in text and illustrations–of the standard document on Fallingwater, the boldest, most personal architectural statement of Wright's mature years, updated with valuable new material from the recently opened Frank Lloyd Wright Archives. "Fascinating"–*The New York Times*. 116 illustrations. 128pp. 9¼ x 10¾. 0-486-27430-6

PHOTOGRAPHIC SKETCHBOOK OF THE CIVIL WAR, Alexander Gardner. 100 photos taken on field during the Civil War. Famous shots of Manassas Harper's Ferry, Lincoln, Richmond, slave pens, etc. 244pp. 10⅝ x 8¼. 0-486-22731-6

FIVE ACRES AND INDEPENDENCE, Maurice G. Kains. Great back-to-the-land classic explains basics of self-sufficient farming. The one book to get. 95 illustrations. 397pp. 5⅜ x 8½. 0-486-20974-1

CATALOG OF DOVER BOOKS

A MODERN HERBAL, Margaret Grieve. Much the fullest, most exact, most useful compilation of herbal material. Gigantic alphabetical encyclopedia, from aconite to zedoary, gives botanical information, medical properties, folklore, economic uses, much else. Indispensable to serious reader. 161 illustrations. 888pp. 6½ x 9¼. 2-vol. set. (Available in U.S. only.)   Vol. I: 0-486-22798-7   Vol. II: 0-486-22799-5

HIDDEN TREASURE MAZE BOOK, Dave Phillips. Solve 34 challenging mazes accompanied by heroic tales of adventure. Evil dragons, people-eating plants, blood-thirsty giants, many more dangerous adversaries lurk at every twist and turn. 34 mazes, stories, solutions. 48pp. 8¼ x 11.   0-486-24566-7

LETTERS OF W. A. MOZART, Wolfgang A. Mozart. Remarkable letters show bawdy wit, humor, imagination, musical insights, contemporary musical world; includes some letters from Leopold Mozart. 276pp. 5⅜ x 8½.   0-486-22859-2

BASIC PRINCIPLES OF CLASSICAL BALLET, Agrippina Vaganova. Great Russian theoretician, teacher explains methods for teaching classical ballet. 118 illus-trations. 175pp. 5⅜ x 8½.   0-486-22036-2

THE JUMPING FROG, Mark Twain. Revenge edition. The original story of The Celebrated Jumping Frog of Calaveras County, a hapless French translation, and Twain's hilarious "retranslation" from the French. 12 illustrations. 66pp. 5⅜ x 8½.   0-486-22686-7

BEST REMEMBERED POEMS, Martin Gardner (ed.). The 126 poems in this superb collection of 19th- and 20th-century British and American verse range from Shelley's "To a Skylark" to the impassioned "Renascence" of Edna St. Vincent Millay and to Edward Lear's whimsical "The Owl and the Pussycat." 224pp. 5⅜ x 8½.   0-486-27165-X

COMPLETE SONNETS, William Shakespeare. Over 150 exquisite poems deal with love, friendship, the tyranny of time, beauty's evanescence, death and other themes in language of remarkable power, precision and beauty. Glossary of archaic terms. 80pp. 5³⁄₁₆ x 8¼.   0-486-26686-9

HISTORIC HOMES OF THE AMERICAN PRESIDENTS, Second, Revised Edition, Irvin Haas. A traveler's guide to American Presidential homes, most open to the public, depicting and describing homes occupied by every American President from George Washington to George Bush. With visiting hours, admission charges, travel routes. 175 photographs. Index. 160pp. 8¼ x 11.   0-486-26751-2

THE WIT AND HUMOR OF OSCAR WILDE, Alvin Redman (ed.). More than 1,000 ripostes, paradoxes, wisecracks: Work is the curse of the drinking classes; I can resist everything except temptation; etc. 258pp. 5⅜ x 8½.   0-486-20602-5

SHAKESPEARE LEXICON AND QUOTATION DICTIONARY, Alexander Schmidt. Full definitions, locations, shades of meaning in every word in plays and poems. More than 50,000 exact quotations. 1,485pp. 6½ x 9¼. 2-vol. set.
                Vol. 1: 0-486-22726-X   Vol. 2: 0-486-22727-8

SELECTED POEMS, Emily Dickinson. Over 100 best-known, best-loved poems by one of America's foremost poets, reprinted from authoritative early editions. No comparable edition at this price. Index of first lines. 64pp. 5³⁄₁₆ x 8¼.   0-486-26466-1

THE INSIDIOUS DR. FU-MANCHU, Sax Rohmer. The first of the popular mys-tery series introduces a pair of English detectives to their archnemesis, the diabolical Dr. Fu-Manchu. Flavorful atmosphere, fast-paced action, and colorful characters enliven this classic of the genre. 208pp. 5³⁄₁₆ x 8¼.   0-486-29898-1

CATALOG OF DOVER BOOKS

THE MALLEUS MALEFICARUM OF KRAMER AND SPRENGER, translated by Montague Summers. Full text of most important witchhunter's "bible," used by both Catholics and Protestants. 278pp. 6⅝ x 10.		0-486-22802-9

SPANISH STORIES/CUENTOS ESPAÑOLES: A Dual-Language Book, Angel Flores (ed.). Unique format offers 13 great stories in Spanish by Cervantes, Borges, others. Faithful English translations on facing pages. 352pp. 5⅜ x 8½.
0-486-25399-6

GARDEN CITY, LONG ISLAND, IN EARLY PHOTOGRAPHS, 1869–1919, Mildred H. Smith. Handsome treasury of 118 vintage pictures, accompanied by carefully researched captions, document the Garden City Hotel fire (1899), the Vanderbilt Cup Race (1908), the first airmail flight departing from the Nassau Boulevard Aerodrome (1911), and much more. 96pp. 8⅞ x 11¾.		0-486-40669-5

OLD QUEENS, N.Y., IN EARLY PHOTOGRAPHS, Vincent F. Seyfried and William Asadorian. Over 160 rare photographs of Maspeth, Jamaica, Jackson Heights, and other areas. Vintage views of DeWitt Clinton mansion, 1939 World's Fair and more. Captions. 192pp. 8⅞ x 11.		0-486-26358-4

CAPTURED BY THE INDIANS: 15 Firsthand Accounts, 1750-1870, Frederick Drimmer. Astounding true historical accounts of grisly torture, bloody conflicts, relentless pursuits, miraculous escapes and more, by people who lived to tell the tale. 384pp. 5⅜ x 8½.		0-486-24901-8

THE WORLD'S GREAT SPEECHES (Fourth Enlarged Edition), Lewis Copeland, Lawrence W. Lamm, and Stephen J. McKenna. Nearly 300 speeches provide public speakers with a wealth of updated quotes and inspiration–from Pericles' funeral oration and William Jennings Bryan's "Cross of Gold Speech" to Malcolm X's powerful words on the Black Revolution and Earl of Spenser's tribute to his sister, Diana, Princess of Wales. 944pp. 5⅜ x 8⅜.		0-486-40903-1

THE BOOK OF THE SWORD, Sir Richard F. Burton. Great Victorian scholar/adventurer's eloquent, erudite history of the "queen of weapons"–from prehistory to early Roman Empire. Evolution and development of early swords, variations (sabre, broadsword, cutlass, scimitar, etc.), much more. 336pp. 6⅛ x 9¼.
0-486-25434-8

AUTOBIOGRAPHY: The Story of My Experiments with Truth, Mohandas K. Gandhi. Boyhood, legal studies, purification, the growth of the Satyagraha (nonviolent protest) movement. Critical, inspiring work of the man responsible for the freedom of India. 480pp. 5⅜ x 8½. (Available in U.S. only.)		0-486-24593-4

CELTIC MYTHS AND LEGENDS, T. W. Rolleston. Masterful retelling of Irish and Welsh stories and tales. Cuchulain, King Arthur, Deirdre, the Grail, many more. First paperback edition. 58 full-page illustrations. 512pp. 5⅜ x 8½.		0-486-26507-2

THE PRINCIPLES OF PSYCHOLOGY, William James. Famous long course complete, unabridged. Stream of thought, time perception, memory, experimental methods; great work decades ahead of its time. 94 figures. 1,391pp. 5⅜ x 8½. 2-vol. set.
Vol. I: 0-486-20381-6		Vol. II: 0-486-20382-4

THE WORLD AS WILL AND REPRESENTATION, Arthur Schopenhauer. Definitive English translation of Schopenhauer's life work, correcting more than 1,000 errors, omissions in earlier translations. Translated by E. F. J. Payne. Total of 1,269pp. 5⅜ x 8½. 2-vol. set.		Vol. 1: 0-486-21761-2		Vol. 2: 0-486-21762-0

CATALOG OF DOVER BOOKS

MAGIC AND MYSTERY IN TIBET, Madame Alexandra David-Neel. Experiences among lamas, magicians, sages, sorcerers, Bonpa wizards. A true psychic discovery. 32 illustrations. 321pp. 5⅜ x 8½. (Available in U.S. only.) 0-486-22682-4

THE EGYPTIAN BOOK OF THE DEAD, E. A. Wallis Budge. Complete reproduction of Ani's papyrus, finest ever found. Full hieroglyphic text, interlinear transliteration, word-for-word translation, smooth translation. 533pp. 6½ x 9¼.
0-486-21866-X

HISTORIC COSTUME IN PICTURES, Braun & Schneider. Over 1,450 costumed figures in clearly detailed engravings–from dawn of civilization to end of 19th century. Captions. Many folk costumes. 256pp. 8⅜ x 11¾. 0-486-23150-X

MATHEMATICS FOR THE NONMATHEMATICIAN, Morris Kline. Detailed, college-level treatment of mathematics in cultural and historical context, with numerous exercises. Recommended Reading Lists. Tables. Numerous figures. 641pp. 5⅜ x 8½.
0-486-24823-2

PROBABILISTIC METHODS IN THE THEORY OF STRUCTURES, Isaac Elishakoff. Well-written introduction covers the elements of the theory of probability from two or more random variables, the reliability of such multivariable structures, the theory of random function, Monte Carlo methods of treating problems incapable of exact solution, and more. Examples. 502pp. 5⅜ x 8½. 0-486-40691-1

THE RIME OF THE ANCIENT MARINER, Gustave Doré, S. T. Coleridge. Doré's finest work; 34 plates capture moods, subtleties of poem. Flawless full-size reproductions printed on facing pages with authoritative text of poem. "Beautiful. Simply beautiful."–*Publisher's Weekly.* 77pp. 9¼ x 12. 0-486-22305-1

SCULPTURE: Principles and Practice, Louis Slobodkin. Step-by-step approach to clay, plaster, metals, stone; classical and modern. 253 drawings, photos. 255pp. 8⅛ x 11.
0-486-22960-2

THE INFLUENCE OF SEA POWER UPON HISTORY, 1660–1783, A. T. Mahan. Influential classic of naval history and tactics still used as text in war colleges. First paperback edition. 4 maps. 24 battle plans. 640pp. 5⅜ x 8½. 0-486-25509-3

THE STORY OF THE TITANIC AS TOLD BY ITS SURVIVORS, Jack Winocour (ed.). What it was really like. Panic, despair, shocking inefficiency, and a little heroism. More thrilling than any fictional account. 26 illustrations. 320pp. 5⅜ x 8½.
0-486-20610-6

ONE TWO THREE . . . INFINITY: Facts and Speculations of Science, George Gamow. Great physicist's fascinating, readable overview of contemporary science: number theory, relativity, fourth dimension, entropy, genes, atomic structure, much more. 128 illustrations. Index. 352pp. 5⅜ x 8½. 0-486-25664-2

DALÍ ON MODERN ART: The Cuckolds of Antiquated Modern Art, Salvador Dalí. Influential painter skewers modern art and its practitioners. Outrageous evaluations of Picasso, Cézanne, Turner, more. 15 renderings of paintings discussed. 44 calligraphic decorations by Dalí. 96pp. 5⅜ x 8½. (Available in U.S. only.) 0-486-29220-7

ANTIQUE PLAYING CARDS: A Pictorial History, Henry René D'Allemagne. Over 900 elaborate, decorative images from rare playing cards (14th–20th centuries): Bacchus, death, dancing dogs, hunting scenes, royal coats of arms, players cheating, much more. 96pp. 9¼ x 12¼. 0-486-29265-7

MAKING FURNITURE MASTERPIECES: 30 Projects with Measured Drawings, Franklin H. Gottshall. Step-by-step instructions, illustrations for constructing handsome, useful pieces, among them a Sheraton desk, Chippendale chair, Spanish desk, Queen Anne table and a William and Mary dressing mirror. 224pp. 8⅛ x 11¼. 0-486-29338-6

NORTH AMERICAN INDIAN DESIGNS FOR ARTISTS AND CRAFTSPEOPLE, Eva Wilson. Over 360 authentic copyright-free designs adapted from Navajo blankets, Hopi pottery, Sioux buffalo hides, more. Geometrics, symbolic figures, plant and animal motifs, etc. 128pp. 8⅜ x 11. (Not for sale in the United Kingdom.) 0-486-25341-4

THE FOSSIL BOOK: A Record of Prehistoric Life, Patricia V. Rich et al. Profusely illustrated definitive guide covers everything from single-celled organisms and dinosaurs to birds and mammals and the interplay between climate and man. Over 1,500 illustrations. 760pp. 7½ x 10⅛. 0-486-29371-8

VICTORIAN ARCHITECTURAL DETAILS: Designs for Over 700 Stairs, Mantels, Doors, Windows, Cornices, Porches, and Other Decorative Elements, A. J. Bicknell & Company. Everything from dormer windows and piazzas to balconies and gable ornaments. Also includes elevations and floor plans for handsome, private residences and commercial structures. 80pp. 9⅜ x 12¼. 0-486-44015-X

WESTERN ISLAMIC ARCHITECTURE: A Concise Introduction, John D. Hoag. Profusely illustrated critical appraisal compares and contrasts Islamic mosques and palaces–from Spain and Egypt to other areas in the Middle East. 139 illustrations. 128pp. 6 x 9. 0-486-43760-4

CHINESE ARCHITECTURE: A Pictorial History, Liang Ssu-ch'eng. More than 240 rare photographs and drawings depict temples, pagodas, tombs, bridges, and imperial palaces comprising much of China's architectural heritage. 152 halftones, 94 diagrams. 232pp. 10¾ x 9⅞. 0-486-43999-2

THE RENAISSANCE: Studies in Art and Poetry, Walter Pater. One of the most talked-about books of the 19th century, *The Renaissance* combines scholarship and philosophy in an innovative work of cultural criticism that examines the achievements of Botticelli, Leonardo, Michelangelo, and other artists. "The holy writ of beauty."–Oscar Wilde. 160pp. 5⅜ x 8½. 0-486-44025-7

A TREATISE ON PAINTING, Leonardo da Vinci. The great Renaissance artist's practical advice on drawing and painting techniques covers anatomy, perspective, composition, light and shadow, and color. A classic of art instruction, it features 48 drawings by Nicholas Poussin and Leon Battista Alberti. 192pp. 5⅜ x 8½. 0-486-44155-5

THE MIND OF LEONARDO DA VINCI, Edward McCurdy. More than just a biography, this classic study by a distinguished historian draws upon Leonardo's extensive writings to offer numerous demonstrations of the Renaissance master's achievements, not only in sculpture and painting, but also in music, engineering, and even experimental aviation. 384pp. 5⅜ x 8½. 0-486-44142-3

WASHINGTON IRVING'S RIP VAN WINKLE, Illustrated by Arthur Rackham. Lovely prints that established artist as a leading illustrator of the time and forever etched into the popular imagination a classic of Catskill lore. 51 full-color plates. 80pp. 8⅜ x 11. 0-486-44242-X

HENSCHE ON PAINTING, John W. Robichaux. Basic painting philosophy and methodology of a great teacher, as expounded in his famous classes and workshops on Cape Cod. 7 illustrations in color on covers. 80pp. 5⅜ x 8½. 0-486-43728-0

LIGHT AND SHADE: A Classic Approach to Three-Dimensional Drawing, Mrs. Mary P. Merrifield. Handy reference clearly demonstrates principles of light and shade by revealing effects of common daylight, sunshine, and candle or artificial light on geometrical solids. 13 plates. 64pp. 5⅜ x 8½. 0-486-44143-1

ASTROLOGY AND ASTRONOMY: A Pictorial Archive of Signs and Symbols, Ernst and Johanna Lehner. Treasure trove of stories, lore, and myth, accompanied by more than 300 rare illustrations of planets, the Milky Way, signs of the zodiac, comets, meteors, and other astronomical phenomena. 192pp. 8⅜ x 11. 0-486-43981-X

JEWELRY MAKING: Techniques for Metal, Tim McCreight. Easy-to-follow instructions and carefully executed illustrations describe tools and techniques, use of gems and enamels, wire inlay, casting, and other topics. 72 line illustrations and diagrams. 176pp. 8¼ x 10⅞. 0-486-44043-5

MAKING BIRDHOUSES: Easy and Advanced Projects, Gladstone Califf. Easy-to-follow instructions include diagrams for everything from a one-room house for bluebirds to a forty-two-room structure for purple martins. 56 plates; 4 figures. 80pp. 8¾ x 6⅜. 0-486-44183-0

LITTLE BOOK OF LOG CABINS: How to Build and Furnish Them, William S. Wicks. Handy how-to manual, with instructions and illustrations for building cabins in the Adirondack style, fireplaces, stairways, furniture, beamed ceilings, and more. 102 line drawings. 96pp. 8¾ x 6⅜. 0-486-44259-4

THE SEASONS OF AMERICA PAST, Eric Sloane. From "sugaring time" and strawberry picking to Indian summer and fall harvest, a whole year's activities described in charming prose and enhanced with 79 of the author's own illustrations. 160pp. 8¼ x 11. 0-486-44220-9

THE METROPOLIS OF TOMORROW, Hugh Ferriss. Generous, prophetic vision of the metropolis of the future, as perceived in 1929. Powerful illustrations of towering structures, wide avenues, and rooftop parks–all features in many of today's modern cities. 59 illustrations. 144pp. 8¼ x 11. 0-486-43727-2

THE PATH TO ROME, Hilaire Belloc. This 1902 memoir abounds in lively vignettes from a vanished time, recounting a pilgrimage on foot across the Alps and Apennines in order to "see all Europe which the Christian Faith has saved." 77 of the author's original line drawings complement his sparkling prose. 272pp. 5⅜ x 8½. 0-486-44001-X

THE HISTORY OF RASSELAS: Prince of Abissinia, Samuel Johnson. Distinguished English writer attacks eighteenth-century optimism and man's unrealistic estimates of what life has to offer. 112pp. 5⅜ x 8½. 0-486-44094-X

A VOYAGE TO ARCTURUS, David Lindsay. A brilliant flight of pure fancy, where wild creatures crowd the fantastic landscape and demented torturers dominate victims with their bizarre mental powers. 272pp. 5⅜ x 8½. 0-486-44198-9

Paperbound unless otherwise indicated. Available at your book dealer, online at **www.doverpublications.com**, or by writing to Dept. GI, Dover Publications, Inc., 31 East 2nd Street, Mineola, NY 11501. For current price information or for free catalogs (please indicate field of interest), write to Dover Publications or log on to **www.doverpublications.com** and see every Dover book in print. Dover publishes more than 500 books each year on science, elementary and advanced mathematics, biology, music, art, literary history, social sciences, and other areas.